AIMS AND AIDS

FOR

Girls and Young Women,

ON THE

VARIOUS DUTIES OF LIFE,

INCLUDING

PHYSICAL, INTELLECTUAL, AND MORAL DEVELOPMENT; SELF-CULTURE, IMPROVEMENT, DRESS, BEAUTY, FASHION, EMPLOYMENT, EDUCATION, THE HOME RELATIONS, THEIR DUTIES TO YOUNG MEN, MARRIAGE, WOMANHOOD AND HAPPINESS.

BY REV. G. S. WEAVER,

AUTHOR OF "HOPES AND HELPS," "MENTAL SCIENCE," "WAYS OF LIFE," ETC.

NEW YORK:

FOWLER AND WELLS, PUBLISHERS,

308 BROADWAY.

London: William Horsell, 492 Oxford Street.

BOSTON: 142 Washington-st. | 1856. | PHILADELPHIA: No. 231 Arch-street.

DAVIES AND ROBERTS, STEREOTYPERS,
201 William Street, New York.

PREFACE.

My interest in woman and our common humanity is my only apology for writing this book. I see multitudes of young women about me, whose general training is so deficient in all that pertains to the best ideas of life, and whose aims and efforts are so unworthy of their powers of mind and heart, that I can not make peace with my own conscience without doing something to elevate their aims and quicken their aspirations for the good and pure in thought and life. Our female schools are but poor apologies for the purposes of mind-culture and soul-development. The idea of life they inspire is but a skeleton of custom-service and fashion-worship. It is altogether subservient to what is, not what should be. Society does little else than to teach its girls to be dolls and drudges. The prevailing current of instruction and influence is deplorably low. I feel confident that the best part of society is longing for something better. To obtain it, each one has but to live out, and express to the world his idea of a true life.

In regard to the book I may say, whatever it lacks it has the merit of being in earnest. I hope those who see its deficiencies will make haste to supply them in some form of instruction or encouragement to the class the book addresses. Thinking fathers and mothers and teachers will not complain of this humble effort to serve their daughters and pupils, but will rather add more in a similar direction, and seek to complete what I have endeavored to begin. While life is spared, I hope to work in this field, that my own daughters, as well as those of others, may attain a worthy womanhood.

G. S. W.

St. Louis, 1855.

CONTENTS.

Lecture One.

GIRLHOOD.

Lecture Two.

BEAUTY.

Lecture Three.

DRESS.

Lecture Eight.

EMPLOYMENT.

Lecture Nine.

HOME.

Lecture Ten.

THE RELATIONS AND DUTIES OF YOUNG WOMEN TO YOUNG MEN.

Lecture Eleven.

MARRIAGE.

Lecture Twelve.

RELIGIOUS DUTIES.

AIMS AND AIDS.

Lecture One.

GIRLHOOD.

Angels view Girlhood with Solicitude and Delight—Beauty no perpetual Pledge of Safety—Nothing in Man or Things impels a provident Regard for it—Blossoming Womanhood an Object of deep Interest and Pity—Girlhood's first Work is to Form a Character—It should be *Pure* and *Energetic*—Woman only a Thing—Her Education progressing—Physical Health should be Preserved—A Woman not Herself without Physical Strength—Woman must be Independent, and Earn her own Livelihood—Character must Embody Itself in an Outward Form to be of Service to the World.

If the angels look down upon earth and behold any natural object with especial delight, it must be Girlhood. And yet if they are not gifted with prophetic vision, they must tremble with fearful solicitude while they gaze delighted. There is a fearfulness in the beauty of Girlhood which mingles anxiety in the cup of admiration. No good being can look upon it without casting a solicitous thought forward to its future, to ask whether it will be well or ill with it. The beauty of Girlhood is no perpetual pledge of its safety. Society has built no wall of protection around it. It has no sure defense within itself. Its

1*

Maker has hung no flaming sword turning every way above it to ward off danger. There is nothing in the world of man and things which impels a provident regard for it. Suns, winds, frosts, storms, time, diseases, and death pay no deferential respect to it. Man respects it, bows to it, but while he does it, it withers under his devotion, so little does he mingle wisdom and care in his regard. Society professes to respect it, and so it does, but it subjects it to so many untimely trials and injurious customs, that that very respect is fearful. A young girl, fresh from childhood, blossoming into a woman, rosy health in her veins, innocence in her heart, caroling gayety in her laugh, buoyant life in her step, the rich glance of an opening soul in her eye, grace in her form with the casket of mind richly jeweled, is indeed an object of beauty. He who can behold it and not feel a benevolent interest in it, is an object of pity. He who can live and not live in part for Girlhood, is devoid of the highest order of feeling. He who can see it wither under unrighteous customs or pass away by the blight of unholy abuses, and not drop a tear of sympathy, is less than a generous man. He who sees its perilous position and lifts not his warning voice, fails in a great duty. It is not enough to admire Girlhood; it is not enough to do it graceful honors, make it obsequious bows, strew its pathway with flattering compliments, and call it by all beautiful names. Such outward expressions, unless most judiciously made, are quite as likely to do it injury as direct abuse. Girlhood is full of tenderness and weakness. The germs of its future strength are its most perilous weaknesses now. Its mightiest energies often kindle the fires of its ruin. Its most salient points of character are often soonest invaded. Indeed, it can scarcely be said to have a character. It is forming one, but knows not yet what it will be. Its interior now is not exactly a chaos, but a beautiful disorder. The elements of something grand are there, but they are not yet polished nor put together, nor compactly cemented. This work is yet to be done. It is the great work of Girlhood. It is the moral art to which it is to apply all its ingenuity and energy. Girlhood is not all a holiday season; it is more a working time, a study hour, an apprenticeship. True, it has buoyant spirits, and should let them out with fresh good-will at proper times. It has its playful moods, which should not only be indulged but encouraged, but not wholly for the sake of the momentary enjoyment, but rather to infuse the forming character largely with the element of cheerfulness. A gloomy Girlhood is as odd and improper as it is unnatural. And it is improper, not only because it is out of place and wrong, but because it shades the character with a desponding hue. Desponding is absolutely wrong in itself. It is a perversion of our minds. To put on weeds when nobody is dead, to weep when it would be more becoming and useful to laugh, to wear a face of woe when the sunshine of gladness has the best right to preside in our sky, is all wrong. It is absolutely wicked, because it casts a baneful influence upon all with whom we associate, and prepares us to go through life like a frowning cloud or a drooping willow, shading the circle of our influence with melancholic gloom. No, better sing with the birds and laugh with the babbling brooklets than be gloomy in Girlhood. Trials and troubles of course will come. We must sometimes weep, and when we do, it should be done with chastened spirits for real sorrow, that we may be the calmer and happier when we recover from the shock of grief. Such weeping is a gracious and healthy exercise. It does not check the true joyousness of Girlhood's nature, nor cast any darkening line into the future character. April suns are all the brighter for April showers. The real sorrows ordinarily incident to Girlhood are not many; the real causes for gloom are few; the most are imaginary. This is true of all ages. Our *borrowed* trouble is much more than that which comes as our own in the legitimate course of our life. Trouble is the worst article we can borrow. We have the least need for it, and it is a miserable dose to take. Of all things which it does, Girlhood should not borrow trouble. A heavy interest will have to be paid for it in the future; and there is danger that it will make the soul absolutely bankrupt. If borrowed trouble would go home when we told it to, and would never leave a track behind, it would do less injury. But it will not. It is hard to get rid of, and always leaves its dark trail on the most beautiful feelings of the heart. If Girlhood is mindful of any thing, it should be of the shadows that fall upon the heart. Whether they be of delusion, disappointment, or sin, they are bad, and will make sad marks in the character to be borne through life. Age can never forget its youth; nor can one easily rub out dark lines traced in his character in its forming state. If I could speak to Girlhood in its wide realm of beauty and promise all over the world, I should say to it, that its first work is to form a fitting character with which to pass through life and do the great work of woman. There is much in starting right. A stumble in the start often defeats the race, while a good strike at the onset often wins the victory. There is no more alarming feature in the Girlhood of our times than its apparent indifference to the great work before it. Multitudes of girls are as thoughtless and giddy as the lambs that sport on the lea. They seem scarcely to cast a prophetic glance before. They live as though life was a theater, good for nothing but its acting. I know there is much reason why girls do live so, why they are so heedless of the grandeur that swells into eternal glory before them. I know they have been taught by the customs of society, by the follies of their elders, to regard themselves as the playthings of men, the ornaments of society, rather than the helpers of themselves and their race, and the solid substance of the social fabric. But it is time they had learned better. They must soon know that they are made for a purpose as grand as that which brought the Saviour of the world into being. They must soon know that their powers were made for the highest order of usefulness and excellency. They must soon know that if in Girlhood they regard themselves as playthings and pets, in womanhood they will have to be drudges or the cast-off dolls of their boyish husbands, or the hangers-on to a society they would but can not be a part of. Is life a preparation for eternity? so is Girlhood a preparation for womanhood. Do effects follow their causes? so will Girlhood send its life and character into womanhood. If a girl would be a good woman, she must commence now. If she would be wise, she must not frolic away her early life. If she would not feel the hand of oppression in age, she must lay now the foundation of a noble independence which will make her self-reliant, energetic, calm, and persistent in the pursuit of life's great aim. Not only is a *pure* character needed, chastity of thought and feeling, but one of *energy*. It is grand to be pure of heart; it is glorious to be virtuous, to be able to resist temptation and confound all tempters. This, we confess, is one of the prime beauties of female character. But this is not all that is needed. Life is more than a trial of virtue, more a scene of temptation. It is a work. Christ resisted temptation. But that was not all he had to do. That only showed him ready for the great work before him. So woman has something more to do than to beat back the tempter. If she can do this, she proves herself made of the pure gold. She has a mission to engage in, a great work to do. All women have. This work requires that they shall possess *energy* as well as purity. They must have force of will to dare and to do. They must dare to be and do that which is right; dare to face false customs; dare to frown on fashion; dare to resist oppression; dare to assert their rights; dare to be persecuted for righteousness' sake; dare to do their own thinking and acting; dare to be above the silly pride and foolish whims and prudish nonsense that enslave little minds. Woman is now bound hand and foot by custom and law. She is only a thing. She is not a conscious independent personality. She is not recognized as a self-directing, responsible agent. She plays a second part. She is shut out from all the higher aims and opportunities of life. Into no college is she permitted to enter if she would cultivate her mind in the highest walks of science and literature. At the feet of no learned professor may she sit for wisdom. Every profession but the teacher's is barred against her, and in that her services are considered not half at par. She can not get more than half-pay for her labor. In law she is but a ninny; if she is married she is less still, an absolute nonentity; her legal existence is merged in that of her husband—the two become one, and he is that one. Then in the every-day customs of life she is but a child. She is not independent, free, energetic. The sun must not shine upon her; she must not breathe the free air, nor bathe her limbs in the clear stream, nor exercise in a healthful and profitable way. She must not go away from her home without a protector; she must not step into the street after nightfall without a watch; she must trail her dress in the mud if others do; hang her bonnet behind her head if it is the fashion; wear a bodiced waist tight as a vice if the milliner says so, and do and submit to a thousand other things equally absurd and wrong. This is her present position. To rise above this position and be what she is capable of being, be strong in mind and purpose, be resolute in the right, be herself untrammeled by custom or law, so far as any being can be in a good society, it requires the culture of energy in the Girlhood of this age. What was once regarded as a sufficient character for a woman, is not enough now. Women are advancing as well as science, mechanics, and men. Young women should remember this. Once it was thought education enough if a woman could read and write a little. Now, she must know a number of things more. The time is not far distant when she must be educated as well as man. So it is in relation to character. Very soon woman must possess energy, self-reliance, force of will and thought, as well as love, or she will be wanting in the essential elements of a noble womanhood. The woman and wife will be quite different at the commencement of the next century from what they were at the commencement of the last. Do the girls understand this? It must be so. The edict has gone out and can not be withdrawn. Woman hails it with joy. She wishes to improve with the advancing age. She would feel sad and look antiquated if the car of progress left her behind. If a few women of this age could be mesmerized and kept in the magnetic state five hundred years, and then unlocked from the somnambulic fetters, how would they compare with the women of that future age? They would be women still, but in character as much antiquated as in custom. This is to be looked for in the very nature of things. We know that woman's education in the future is to be quite different from what it was in the past. We know that the improvements in science and mechanics are making rapid changes in the nature of the labor of life. Women are fast entering into new fields of labor. Who knows but the sewing, cooking, washing, and much else that woman now does, will in a great measure be done by machinery? If so, woman will be left free to employ herself elsewhere. There must be a change. It will probably be for the better. The change will require the culture of new powers or forces in the female character. Woman will rise, not fall. Her character must rise. The young women ought to know it, and be preparing for it. Is the Girlhood of to-day a fit preparation for the duties that will devolve upon the women of the next generation? Parents ought to ask themselves this question. And all young women should consider it well. The elements of a true female character should be carefully studied. It would be well if some strong hand should write out the moral philosophy of Girlhood as a book for schools and academies as well as families, that every young woman might have line upon line and precept upon precept, in the formation of her character. All desire to possess a true character, but all do not know how to acquire it.

A second duty devolves upon Girlhood. It is to preserve its physical health and strength. The richest mind is of but little avail to the world if locked up in a feeble, sickly body. The noblest character would not half make its impression on the world if it was imprisoned in weakness and barricaded with disease. A woman can not be herself unless she possesses physical as well as mental and moral strength. Girlhood has both beauty and strength. Why may they not be carried into womanhood? Shall not the wife and mother retain the beauty and health of the girl? Shall not the woman retain the physical integrity of the girl? There is no good reason why she shall not. Health and strength were made to be life-lasting, or nearly so. So beauty is a rich gift of the Divine Artist given for life. Why should we dissipate it in an hour? It is ungrateful, impious to do it. We ought to prize and retain it as a divine benefaction. God could as well have made Girlhood ugly as beautiful. His wisdom and love chose to make it a model of grace and elegance. Has he laid a necessity upon woman's nature that this beauty shall last but an hour? Far from it. On the other hand, he has made every provision for its preservation. Why, then, is it not preserved? Simply because Girlhood is not instructed in the science of health or life. And this is not so much the fault of young women as it is of parents and society. We study astronomy in all our schools, but where is a class instructed in the economy of health? True, some go through a text-book on physiology, but how meager is the instruction there gleaned relative to the preservation of health, and how few ever think of putting into practice what they do get! When physiologists say that pure air, much exercise, comfortable and airy dress, frequent bathing, sufficient sleep, a plain, simple diet, and regular habits, with a peaceful and active mind, are essential to health, how many young women heed the instruction? Now of what avail will a good character be without health to apply its forces to the work of life? Of what avail is a good boiler and a high pressure of steam to the engineer if his engine is all out of order, so that it has neither strength nor freedom to work? So it is with a good character in a fragile, broken-down body. If there was any other way to use the forces of a good character than through the medium of a physical engine, health would not be a matter of so much importance; but as there is not, it is clear that for all the active, benevolent, and useful purposes of this life, health is about as important as character. Neither is of much utility alone. A boiler pressed full of steam would be useless without an engine to use and apply its forces, and the engine would be as useless without the boiler. Why, then, is Girlhood so prodigal of its health and strength? Why does it imprison itself in close, hot rooms? Why live on a diet that no brute could bear? Why confine every limb and muscle of its body? Why engirdle its waist in warmth and cordage, and expose its feet to every storm and frost, to mud and snow? It is useless to talk, and preach, and write about the value of a good character unless we couple it with an equally earnest lesson about the value of health. It is useless for Girlhood to be anxious about its moral character unless it is equally anxious about its physical character. If we have no right to cultivate a bad character, we have no right to abuse the only means by which a good character can be of use to the world. If we have no moral right to set a bad example before our fellow-men, we have no right to weaken and disease a good physical organization. And it would be difficult to show the reasoning at fault, should we conclude that we have no more moral right to be sick than we have to sin. But we hope to say more on this subject before our work is done.

Still another duty presses upon Girlhood. It relates to a livelihood, to the practical work of pushing its way through life. Woman must eat, wear, be sheltered, educated, protected, warmed, and amused, as much as any other human being. She can not be thus supplied except by charity or her own labor. It is degrading to accept of all life's necessities at the hand of charity. No woman possessed of a genuine womanly character will do it. The character would forbid that she should do it. She must then be independent, or as much so as any are. She must have some livelihood. She must not only have a good character and good health, but an ability to do something for herself and others. Both character and health would be of little avail if she was a shiftless, homeless, useless know-nothing in relation to all the great activities of life, by which we secure the necessaries and comforts of our existence. It is through useful industry and labor that the rarest beauties and forces of character shine. Men show themselves great and good in their professions and callings. The man whose hands are taught no skill, who is trained to no profession, is a ninny, or nearly so. Why is not a woman who is equally useless? Characters must have some way to embody themselves in an outward form to be of service to the world. The best way is in devotion to some useful calling or profession, by which our powers may be called upon for their best efforts in a direction that shall promise a full reward for ourselves and a good surplus for our fellow-men.

Lecture. Two.

BEAUTY.

God a Lover of Beauty—Every thing in the Universe Beautiful—The Admirer of Beauty should Reverence its Author—The Love of Beauty elevating in its Tendency—Its Abuses Fearful—Man a Part of Nature, and God in all—Woman the most Perfect Type of Beauty—Youthful Woman exposed to great Temptation—Beauty a Charming, but Dangerous Gift—The most Beautiful should be the most Pious—Beauty of Person Worthless without Loveliness of Character—"Strong-minded" Women not Beautiful—Beauty the Nurse of Vanity—Value of Character depreciates with Increase of Beauty when substituted for Moral Worth—Beauty only Skin-deep—Beauty Two-fold: Inward and Outward—Inward Beauty shines through—Beauty of Soul made Washington, Josephine, and Channing glorious—Every Woman may be Beautiful—Cheerfulness, Agreeable Manners, a Correct Taste, and Kindness should be Cultivated.

We doubt not that God is a lover of Beauty. We speak reverently. He fashioned the worlds in Beauty, when there was no eye to behold them but his own. All along the wild old forest he has carved the forms of Beauty. Every cliff, and mountain, and tree is a statue of Beauty. Every leaf, and stem, and vine, and flower is a form of Beauty. Every hill, and dale, and landscape is a picture of Beauty. Every cloud, and mist-wreath, and vapor-vail is a shadowy reflection of Beauty. Every spring and rivulet, lakelet, river, and ocean, is a glassy mirror of Beauty. Every diamond, and rock, and pebbly beach is a mine of Beauty. Every sun, and planet, and star is a blazing face of Beauty. All along the aisles of earth, all over the arches of heaven, all through the expanses of the universe, are scattered in rich and infinite profusion the life-gems of Beauty. All natural motion is Beauty in action The winds, the waves, the clouds, the trees, the birds, the animals, all move beautifully; and beautifully do the joyous light-words of the skies dance their eternal cotillion of glory. From the mote that plays its little frolic in the sunbeam, to the world that blazes along the sapphire spaces of the firmament, are visible the ever-varying features of the enrapturing spirit of Beauty. All this great realm of dazzling and bewildering beauty was made by God. What shall we say then, is he not a lover of Beauty? Is it irreverence thus to speak? No; but rather reverence. What reverent soul does not love to look at God in his works? Go out in the still morning, when the golden gates of day are turning slowly back to let the morning king come in with a great crown of rosy light streaking half around the heavens, on his brow; or at noon, when the whole firmament and the joyous earth are bathed in a golden flood, soft, and warm, and life-inspiring; or at evening, when even the zephyrs are folding up their wings with the little birds, and the trees, and the fields, and the smiling mountain tops are bidding a sweet good-night to their heavenly king as encurtained in diamond glory he sinks to rest; or at night, when the stars come out to keep their vigils over the sleeping earth; go out at such times, and what heart is not bewildered with the sense of Beauty that steals over it like a divine charm? and through that beauty is not carried up to God the beautiful and bountiful author of it all? God hath made every thing beautiful in its time. I envy not him who is undevout in the presence of so much Beauty. How easily can the devout spirit go through nature up to nature's God. Who loves nature should love God. Who admires Beauty should reverence its Author. Natural beauty inspires piety in a good heart. To commune with nature intelligently is to commune with God. Who ever loves a flower, a bird, a landscape view, a rainbow, a star, the blue sky, should love God. God is in them all. He is in the aisles of the forest, the waves of the deep, the solitudes of the mountain, and the fragrance of the green fields. Beauty is of divine origin, and we should admire, ay, and love it too. It should fill us with sweet thoughts of God, with worshipful emotions, with reverent aspirings. The love of Beauty we should cultivate within us as a gift of the good Father, and a shrine at which we may worship him acceptably. He has not given us this delicate sense of Beauty to be neglected. It is our duty to preserve it well and cultivate it diligently. None of us love Beauty too much, if our love is enlightened and devout. He who has no love of Beauty in his soul is a great way from God, and very near the earth, the animal. The love of Beauty is refining and elevating in its tendency. Yet it is too often indulged without a thought of God or a reverent emotion. It is a love which may be united with earthly desires, or with heavenly aspirations. It may lead us downward or upward, according to the use we make of it. It may pander to pride and vanity, lust and appetite, or inspire to virtue, religion, and inward life. It is a love which should be brought within the sphere of moral government as much as the passions of our lower nature. It is a love, too, which perhaps leads as many astray, corrupts as many lives, degrades as many natures, as almost any feeling we possess. Its abuses are fearful in their character and wide in their influence. It is a power of mind lovely to behold, and even when degraded it is like a diamond in the dust. So far as the love of natural things is concerned, there is but little danger of abuse. Nature is always lovely, and always to be admired. She always reminds us of God and our duty; always teaches us our own littleness and frailty, and works upon all our passions a calming subduing influence.

But we may pass from Beauty in nature to Beauty in man. Strictly speaking, man is a part of nature; but by common usage we often speak of nature as distinct from both God and man. Really, man is a part of nature, and God is in it all. Take God away from his works, and where would they be? They would vanish like a body deprived of its soul. Take God out of a flower, and it would wither and vanish in an instant. Take God out of a sun or star, and they would go out as a candle in the wind. Take God out of any thing—a tree, an animal, a man—and it would cease to be. So take God out of nature, and there would be no nature. Not that nature is God, but that there is no nature without God. God is in all things; he pervades, sustains, and moves all things. The laws of nature, of which we often speak, are the arteries and veins which God has made, along which he pours through the great body of his universe the spirit of his infinite being. Man, then, as a part of this nature, is pervaded by God. And here, as elsewhere, he has shown his presence in the surprising Beauty in which he has made his creatures. Yes, man is beautiful; the natural man, undeformed by abuses, is an object of Beauty. We speak of man in the generic sense, as including women also.

Woman, by common consent, we regard as the most perfect type of Beauty on earth. To her we ascribe the highest charms belonging to this wonderful element so profusely mingled in all God's works. Her form is molded and finished in exquisite delicacy of perfection. The earth gives us no form more perfect, no features more symmetrical, no style more chaste, no movements more graceful, no finish more complete; so that our artists ever have and ever will regard the woman-form of humanity as the most perfect earthly type of Beauty. This form is most perfect and symmetrical in the youth of womanhood; so that youthful woman is earth's queen of Beauty. This is true, not only by the common consent of mankind, but also by the strictest rules of scientific criticism.

This being an admitted fact, woman, and especially youthful woman, is laid under strong obligations and exposed to great temptations. Beauty has wonderful charms, and hence it is a dangerous gift. We did not make ourselves physically beautiful. Another hand than ours molded our forms, tinged our faces with the vermilion of life, colored our hair and eyes, bleached our teeth and touched our bodies with that exquisite finish which we call Beauty. Another being than ourselves gave us that mysterious power of mind by which we discern and are charmed by Beauty. Then if Beauty hath charms, if it is a possession which we value, we are under peculiar obligations to its Giver. "Every good and perfect gift cometh down from the Father of lights." This is one. A charming gift conferred for pleasure and profit. Who possesses it should be grateful. Who revels in its charms should be reverent in praise, pure in heart, holy in life, devout in demeanor, beautiful in character. She who is most beautiful should be most moved to a pious character and a useful life. She whose dwelling God hath wrought into the rich fullness of Beauty almost divine, who is spread over with a profusion of charms which no eye can behold without ecstasy, is ungrateful and mean in spirit if she returns not to God the "Beauty of holiness" in her life.

Beauty will not only win for her admiring eyes, but it will win her favor; it will draw *hearts* toward her; it will awaken tender and agreeable feelings in her behalf; it will disarm the stranger of the peculiar prejudices he often has toward those he knows not; it will pave the way to esteem; it will weave the links to friendship's chain; it will throw an air of agreeableness into the manners of all who approach her. All this her Beauty will do for her before she puts forth a single effort of her own to win the esteem and love of her fellows. All this is the direct, immediate, and agreeable result of a gift from her Father in heaven. How, then, should she feel toward that Father? With what noble gifts of gratitude and love should she seek to repay Him for this rich inheritance of Beauty! How useful, how lovely in spirit should she be! how thankful, how pious, how virtuous, how rich in inward charms! These are what God asks in return. Think of it, young women, as it really is. See God clothing your forms with Beauty, rich and ravishing in its charms; see that Beauty winning for you flowery paths of life, softening all hearts that approach you, making it easy, ay, almost a necessity, for them to love and esteem you; think how much you prize it, and how pleasant it is to your friends; and then think what God asks in return for this lovely gift. It is that you should be beautiful inwardly as He has made you outwardly; that you should be grateful, dutiful, merciful, pure in heart and life, meek, loving, useful, and pious. Does He ask more than what is reasonable? Can you do less than to love Him for the rich endowments he has bestowed upon you, less than to obey his commands, imitate his character, seek instruction from his Son, and be kind and good to his children?

How can you look upon your own forms or see your features in a mirror, without thinking of Him who made you thus? How can you look upon any thing beautiful, or contemplate the sense of Beauty within you, without reverent feelings toward God the Giver of all?

What does your Beauty avail you unless you are beautiful in spirit, lovely in character, useful in life? Ah, it is only a mockery, calling reproaches upon you from all the good, and the reproof of Heaven for your ingratitude! One of the most unpleasant, if we may not say hateful, objects in the world, is a cold, vain, heartless, beautiful woman.

I said that Beauty is a dangerous gift. It is even so. Like wealth, it has ruined its thousands. Thousands of the most beautiful women are destitute of common sense and common humanity. No gift from Heaven is so general and so widely abused by woman as the gift of Beauty. In about nine cases in ten it makes her silly, senseless, thoughtless, giddy, vain, proud, frivolous, selfish, low, and mean. I think I have seen more girls spoiled by Beauty than by any other one thing. "She is beautiful, and she knows it," is as much as to say she is spoiled. A beautiful girl is very likely to believe she was made to be looked at; and so she sets herself up for a show at every window, in every door, on every corner of the street, in every company at which opportunity offers for an exhibition of herself. And believing and acting thus, she soon becomes good for nothing else; and when she comes to be a middle-aged woman she is that weakest, most sickening of all human things—a faded Beauty.

It has long since passed into a proverb, that homely women are good, that plain women have strong common sense. An eminent writer asks, "Who ever saw a handsome talented woman?" There is among us a class of "strong-minded women," brave of heart and deep of soul, high of purpose and pure of life, who are stirring the country from heart to circumference by the sterling powers of womanhood which they possess, and there is not "a beauty" among them. There is a large class of female writers in every enlightened country, over the productions of whose genius the world hangs delighted, but there is not "a beauty" wields the magic pen. There are women engaged in great enterprises of benevolence and piety, reformers, missionaries, teachers who labor and live for the causes in which they are engaged, but scarcely a beauty can be found among them all. But why? Is Beauty uncongenial to talent and worth? By no means. But Beauty is a dangerous gift, and few beautiful women ever seek to develop their minds—ever seek to be any thing more than they are. Worth is *made*, not *given*; Beauty is *given*, not *made*. Women who have no Beauty make worth. Those who have Beauty are satisfied with that, and seldom make for themselves much worth. The world has paid court to Beauty, and Beauty has foolishly become satisfied with itself, and been willing to be wooed and petted till it has become the weakest of all weak things. I heard of a man of brilliant talents who is said to have been ruined by the possession of a beautiful head, adorned with a beautiful covering of hair. He was a minister of the Gospel, and entered upon his sacred office with a bright promise of usefulness. He was so much enamored of his own head, that when he walked the street he carried his hat in his hand much of the way, apparently to wipe his forehead, or in seeming thoughtfulness, yet all the while to show his pretty head to the people he met. This weakness soon permeated his whole character, and rendered it vain, imbecile, trifling, and ignoble. In a little while he died a ministerial death—and died of nothing but a beautiful head. God had richly endowed him with brilliant qualities of mind and great beauty of person, and he returned only vanity and weakness for these gifts. Oh, how weak is man! Die of Beauty! Die a moral death, or live a useless, foolish life because he is wickedly vain of God's gifts! Beauty is full often the nurse of vanity, and vanity is the bane of womanhood. I am sorry to say it, and more sorry because it is so. It is a pity that so lovely a gift from the Hand Divine should be so wickedly perverted. Beauty ought to inspire rather than weaken its possessor, ought to elevate rather than depress her. And it would, if woman-life was rightly appreciated, if the woman-soul was rightly taught, and the woman-heart of humanity rightly awakened to its grand capacities and duties. Woman is not alone to blame for this strange and wicked fire kindled on the altar of Beauty. Man is as guilty as she. He has praised Beauty and foolishly smiled upon it. He has chosen it for his companion. He has passed by worth in search of Beauty. So he has helped women to be vain and trifling. He has not sought to ennoble her heart so much as to weaken it with flatteries. And he together with her has suffered as a consequence. Man and woman rise and fall together. What injures or benefits one does the same to the other.

Take fifty of the most beautiful young ladies that any town affords, and put them in one company. You would of course have the belles of the town. What would they talk about? What would they think about? What would they do? They are as richly endowed with mind as any other fifty girls in town, but how would they show it? Only in an exhibition of their personal beauty. You know, young women, that common sense would have to play "hide-and-seek" in that company. You know that follies and trifles, fooleries, fashions, foibles, and failings, would occupy their whole minds. Then let fifty of the young men with whom they are in the habit of associating enter into their company, and what an exhibition of Beauty and display would follow! Not one of them would try so much to show her good sense as her pretty face. Let good sense sit back and look on, and methinks it would be not a little disgusted.

Take fifty of the plainest young women from the same circles in our town, and place them under similar circumstances, and, if I mistake not, their behavior would be much more genteel and becoming, their conversation much more interesting and intelligent, and their feelings much more refined and noble. Am I wrong in this supposition? If I am wrong, I have read woman-life to a poor purpose.

I have often seen sisters, one of whom was plain and the other handsome, and almost invariably I have found the plain one more sensible and kind, less vain and frivolous. Indeed, I have generally found value of character to depreciate with increase of Beauty.

Why is it so? Is Beauty connected with less natural endowments of mind, less kindness of heart? By no means. Is Beauty an evil in itself considered? By no means. Is it morally corrupting? Not of itself. The fault is with those who possess it. They abuse the lovely gift. They attempt to make it answer in the place of good sense. They weigh it against goodness of heart, and find it wofully wanting. They substitute it for moral worth, put it in the place of refinement of manners, try to make it win for them the esteem and love which can be given only to a cultivated and noble spirit. And for all these purposes it utterly fails. Besides this abuse of it, they usually become vain, proud, silly, and frivolous. It need not be so, but it generally is so. I have often noticed that people are not generally so vain of their own attainments as they are of the gifts of God. A beautiful woman is more vain of her beauty than she is of her personal attainments. A talented man is more likely to be vain of his natural talents than of the culture he has given them. A rich singer is more likely to be vain of his voice than of what he has done to train it. So it is generally; we are more apt to be vain of what God does for us than of what we do for ourselves. It is so with the possessor of personal Beauty, and hence beautiful women are so tempted to vanity and a neglect of all useful culture of mind and heart. They think their Beauty will carry them through the world, and they need not strive for worth of character; they may neglect the ordinary means of culture and improvement, forgetting that a good heart, a true life, a cultivated mind, and a noble soul can have no possible substitutes; forgetting that Beauty will soon fade, that nothing makes old age beautiful but worth, and that another life succeeds this that Beauty of body can not enter, and in which Beauty of soul is honored and cherished as of eternal worth.

These facts have long since taught sensible men to beware of beautiful women—to sound them carefully before they give them their confidence. Beauty is shallow—only skin-deep; fleeting—only for a few years' reign; dangerous—tempting to vanity and lightness of mind; deceitful—dazzling often to bewilder; weak—reigning only to ruin; gross—leading often to sensual pleasure. And yet we say it need not be so. Beauty is lovely, and ought to be innocently possessed. It has charms which ought to be used for good purposes. It is a delightful gift, which ought to be received with gratitude and worn with grace and meekness. It should always minister to inward Beauty. Every woman of beautiful form and features should cultivate a beautiful mind and heart.

Beauty is two-fold. It is inward and outward. We have been speaking of outward Beauty. We would now dwell upon inward Beauty—Beauty of spirit, soul, mind, heart, life. There is a Beauty which perishes not. It is such as the angels wear. It forms the whitewashed robes of the saints. It wreathes the countenance of every doer of good. It adorns every *honest* face. It shines in the *virtuous* life. It molds the hands of *charity*. It sweetens the voice of sympathy. It sparkles on the brow of wisdom. It flashes in the eye of love. It breathes in the spirit of piety. It is the Beauty of the heaven of heavens—the Beauty of God and his Son—the Beauty of eternal life," "incorruptible, undefiled, and that fadeth not away." It is not a meteor flashing to deceive; not a glow-worm, shining to fade; not a glitter, leading to bewilder; not a charm, working to tempt. No. It is positive, real, lovely, delightful, glorious, and eternal. It is the life of goodness, the spirit of love, the brilliance of virtue. It is that which may grow by the hand of culture in every human soul. It is the flower of the spirit which blossoms on the tree of life. Every soul may plant and nurture it in its own garden, in its own Eden. It is Eden renewed—Paradise regained. Every one may have an Eden—a garden of Eden in his own soul. That is where the first garden was. It is where the second must be. And that second when complete will be heaven. This is the capacity for Beauty that God has given to the human soul, and this the Beauty placed within the reach of us all. We may all be beautiful. Though our forms may be uncomely and our features not the prettiest, our spirits may be beautiful. And this inward beauty always shines through. A beautiful heart will flash out in the eye. A lovely soul will glow in the face. A sweet spirit will tune the voice and wreathe the countenance in charms. Oh, there is a power in interior Beauty that melts the hardest hearts! I see it in a mother's love; I see it in a sister's tenderness; I see it in the widow's mite of charity; in the wife's bosom of burning truthfulness; in the devotion of the saint; in the strong purpose, the noble resolve, the dauntless ambition for good. I see it in the affectionate home, the congenial companionship, in the trusting heart of friendship, and most of all in the Christian spirit and life. How this beauty wins us, charms us, ravishes our souls. Our hardness all melts before it. Could Washington come here, and we all stand up in his presence, how we should forget the Beauty or ugliness of our forms, and all be moved by the grand and eternal Beauty of his spirit! Could Josephine, the empress of the French, stand in our presence, how the plumes of our vanity would come down and the lightness of our frivolity depart before the charms of her wisdom and virtue! Could the matchless Mrs. Hemans rise before us in her peerless Beauty of soul, how little should we prize the fleeting Beauty of these mortal bodies, and how ashamed should we be of our foolish pride and thoughtlessness! Could we invite before us the departed Channing, Mayo, Weare, and gaze for one little moment at the effulgence of virtue and goodness that made them the charmed centers of their wide circles of influence and usefulness, how mean should we feel that we ever thought so much of our pretty forms and faces, and so little of that Beauty which is a fadeless power and a glorious life in the soul! It was not Beauty of person that made these men and women so glorious in their day, and so grand in the memories of the generations that follow them. It was Beauty of soul. So all about us we have men and women who are living charms in their families and in their circles of associations; but it is not their Beauty of person that makes them so. It is another Beauty, inward, living, powerful, which charges their wisdom, sweetens their actions with love, and tempers their lives with piety. Oh, how lovely it makes them! We gaze upon them with reverence. We never once think of their outward Beauty. No, it would be sacrilege to do so. They have a higher Beauty. We see it playing on their faces; we feel it in the charm of their presence, and hear it in the music of their voices. It is the Beauty of virtue, wisdom, goodness, magnanimity, meekness, piety. There is a cultured finish in their actions, a refined sweetness in their manners, a chastened delicacy and power in their lives which give them their Beauty.

This is the Beauty, young women, to which I would invite your admiring attention. Now, in the May-morning of your lives, you should search for the flowery wreaths of spiritual Beauty. If God has arrayed your persons in the elegance of rich proportions and lively colorings, be thankful, and make this outward Beauty the symbol of one more rich, lasting, and priceless within which you will seek to adorn your minds. If your forms and features are not attractive, then be thoughtful that you may cultivate your minds, enrich your hearts, beautify your spirits, make useful your lives without the temptations of an alluring outward loveliness. Beautiful or not beautiful, it matters little so the mind be cultivated, the heart subdued, and the life right. Nothing is more important to young women than that they should early learn to distinguish between outward and inward attractions, to place a proper estimate upon each. The true woman-beauty is inward; that which makes the woman attractive, lovely, useful, esteemed, loved, and happy, and is deeper than the color on her cheeks or the form of her person. It is in her mind, and is attainable by her own exertions. Every woman may be beautiful. Every young woman may shine, attract, and be admired and loved. She has only to be lovely in spirit and life, to be good and useful, cheerful and agreeable.

Cheerfulness is a Beauty which every body admires. A cheerful spirit is a continual feast. It smiles its way through life. It wins crowns for its possessor. It makes and gives happiness. All sunshine and flowers is a cheerful heart. It shines in perpetual spring. Its birds are ever singing, and its joys ever new. Every young woman may cultivate a cheerful spirit, and throw its charm around her associates. *Agreeable manners* is another Beauty of spirit which charms every body. It is the product of a kind heart and a refined taste. We can not describe it, though we all know what it is. It is one of the charming graces of cultivated womanhood. All who will, may possess it. But they can not do it without effort, culture, and constant watchfulness over the impulses and habits. To possess agreeableness of manners they must have a *correct taste.* This is an inward Beauty of rare loveliness. It grows out of a good judgment and an informed mind. Ignorance and awkwardness are usually found together. Every young woman may inform her mind, enrich her judgment, and thus correct and discipline her taste. She may read; she may think; she may act; she may imitate the good and wise; she may restrain her folly; curb her impulses; subdue her passions; awaken good aspirations, and thus by persevering effort she may acquire a correct taste.

Then she may cultivate *kindness of heart.* She may seek to do good to all, to feel for their sufferings, pity their weakness, assuage their griefs, assist them in their trials, and breath everywhere the spirit of a kind heart.

Thus she may make herself beautiful in spirit. And she may rest assured that that Beauty will win her laurels of life and joy. It will soon become apparent to all with whom she associates. It will come out and sit like a queen on her person. It will speak in all her words and actions. She will move amid enchantment. No deformity of body can conceal a beautiful spirit. It will shine through an ugly face, a shriveled form, a bad complexion. Nothing made of clay can hide it. No beauty of person can conceal deformity of spirit. A bad temper will look hateful in the prettiest face. A hollow heart will sound its dirge of woe through the most perfectly organized form. Peering through all outward Beauty is seen the hateful demon of a bad heart. Shining through all bodily deformity are always visible the angel faces of the virtues that cluster in a beautiful spirit. All wise young women will rest not till they possess the Beauty of spirit.

Lecture Three.

DRESS.

Religion and Dress—Variety in Nature—Dress should not be Injurious—Present Customs Unhealthy, Slovenly, and Immodest—A Subject of Religious Consideration—Suicide *vs.* Providence—Foolish Vanity—Taste an Element of Mind—Dress should be Symbolical—Woman should Elevate her Aims—Appropriate Dress Admirable.

COMFORT, taste, and religion agree that *Dress* is one of the proprieties of civilized and Christian life. If religion reaches a part, it does the whole of life. If it should direct us anywhere, it should in the matter of Dress. There are few things upon which people are more liable to err, and about which there is more wrong feeling than this. Many religious sects have seen this, and have attempted to bring the matter of Dress wholly under the ban of ecclesiastical direction. In this they were partly right and partly in error. They were right in believing that religion should extend a fostering and restraining care over the subject of Dress; but wrong in believing that it should Dress all in the same manner. Our Quaker brethren, the Friends, than whom no purer and better people have ever lived—noble followers of the lowly Prince of Peace—the truest *friends* that humanity has ever found since the days of the Apostles, or that Jesus has ever had in the earth—the world-renowned speakers of the sweet, plain language which hath the charm of divinity within it, and in which love always chooses to express its tender emotions—adopted the idea that religion should extend its sway over the subject of Dress. In this they did well; but, in my humble opinion, erred in putting the shears into the hands of sectarianism to cut every man's Dress by exactly the same pattern, and to choose it all from the same grand web of drab. It is sectarianism, and not religion, which would Dress every man alike. That is making Dress the badge of the order. Any thing put on outwardly to tell the world to what sect you belong is an evidence of sectarianism, and not of religion. The Quaker wears the sign of his sect all over his body. The drunkard wears his on his face. The Catholic wears his in his beads and cross. If God had designed that all men should dress in one color, methinks he would have made them all of one complexion; and not only so, but would have colored nature in that peculiar hue—would have clothed all the forests, fields, flowers, birds, and skies in that color, and have fitted every man's taste to enjoy it.

If He had designed every man to cut his Dress in one form, after one model, I see not why he did not fashion nature after that pattern, and make that peculiar curve, and cast the grand leading ones in all his works, and fit the universal taste to that form. But, on the contrary, nature is robed in every variety of color and form; the human taste is equally diversified, and the forms and complexions of men are not less various.

It is clear to my mind that we may reason from this, that men not only may, but should dress in different forms and colors and after differing styles. What is pleasing to some men's taste is and ever will be displeasing to others. Taste is an inherent quality in our minds. We naturally possess tastes peculiar to ourselves, and no amount of culture can make these differing tastes agreeably harmonious. Some tastes revel in the gay, others in the grave, others in the changing. Some delight in high colors, others in subdued; some in diversity, others in sameness. There is nothing irreligious in this difference in taste. Each one is equally gratified in God's beautiful and diversified works. The grave and golden clouds, the dark and rosy tints of the sunset sky, the gorgeous rainbow and the modest Aurora, the flashing flower and the lowly heather, the towering pine and the creeping vine, the rich green field of summer and the calm gray forest of winter, the thousand million forms of the hill-and-dale landscape, and the equally diversified colors and forms of birds and beasts, confer the richest feasts of pleasure upon every variety of natural taste.

Looking thus upon the panoramic field of God's works, we must conclude that he has taken especial care to gratify the varying tastes of his creatures. And more than this; we must conclude that He himself has an infinite taste, which finds an infinite pleasure in making and viewing this magnificent universe of flashing splendor and somber sweetness, this field on field, system beyond system, far off where human eye can never reach, all shining and moving in an infinite variety of forms, colors and movements. Moreover, we can not but feel that God is a lover of Dress. He has put on robes of beauty and glory upon all his works. Every flower is dressed in richness; every field blushes beneath a mantle of beauty; every star is vailed in brightness; every bird is clothed in the habiliments of the most exquisite taste. The cattle upon the thousand hills are dressed by the Hand Divine. Who, studying God in his works, can doubt that he will smile upon the evidence of correct taste manifested by his children in clothing the forms he has made them? Who can doubt that Dress is a matter properly coming within purview of religion? Religion is what we learn of God. It is human imitation of the Divinity. "Be ye perfect, as your Father in heaven is perfect."

Now what I mean by Dress coming under the direction of religion is, that our manners and style of Dress shall not interfere with the principles of true religion, shall not injure the body, corrupt the heart, debase the mind of the individual; shall not degrade society, nor work any evil influence in it, but, on the contrary, shall do good both to the individual and society. Now let us ask whether our present modes of Dress are thus brought under the direction of religious principles?

First: Do our modes of Dress injure our bodies? In this, young women, you may be judges. Are your forms permitted to expand as God designed them? Are your organs and limbs and muscles permitted their full and proper play? Is your blood in no way impeded in its life-mission through your bodies? Are you protected from the winter's cold, from wind and wet at all points, as you should be? Can you breathe freely and easily the proper amount of air to oxygenate your blood and give you health and strength? If so, what mean the languid faces, the sallow countenances, the pale cheeks, the wasp-like forms, the rounded shoulders, the bent spines, the feeble lungs, the short breathings, the cold feet, the hampered step, the neuralgic pains, the hysteric nervousness, the weak sides, the frailty, weakness, and painfulness so prevalent among women? What mean the headaches, and liver-complaints, and consumptions, and neuralgias, and the troublesome ailments of your sex from which scarcely a woman of you is free? Those strings which bind so closely your chests, do they not impede your breathing, and thus weaken your lungs and corrupt your systems? Those dresses hooked so closely that every seam in them gapes as in agony, giving you so much the appearance of convicts in strait jackets, are they not in the way when you want to breathe a full breath, and do they permit the exercise of all the muscles that strive for life within them? That enormous weight of skirts that you hang over portions of your bodies that should be choicely protected instead of burdened, how they hang down like so many dead weights on your vitality, weakening and diseasing the most delicate economy of your fearfully and wonderfully made systems! and how your whole frames are taxed every day of your lives with this wrongly placed and worse than useless burden This alone is enough to bring premature disease and death to any ordinary woman. The law of health de mands that the extremities of our bodies should be kep warm and well protected, while the parts containing our vital economy should be only comfortably clothed and left free to the most natural and easy action, well ventilated or exposed to the ingress and egress of the atmosphere, without any local pressures or means for unnatural warmth. Only think of wearing a thick, heavy girdle of many pounds' weight around the whole zone of the abdominal region—a sort of engirdling poultice, heating and pressing like a girdle of hot lava, day after day and year after year! Is it a wonder that you have so many weaknesses and pains and saddening afflictions upon you? And then your feet treading these cold pavements, this damp earth, these frozen or wet walks, in slippers and silk or cotton stockings! The very part of your bodies of all others you should keep most warm and dry, you expose to every wind and frost, water-pool and snow-storm, in the year; sit through the whole winter with them on cold floors, where every door-crack and floor-crack is breathing in upon them cold, damp breaths from cellars or streets while perhaps your heads are hot in a dry stove air, and your lungs are breathing an atmosphere so hot and close that it has scarcely a breath of life in it, and all the while you say you are comfortably dressed!

And then, to make the matter still worse, you trail your

bedrabbled dress into all the mud and water and tobacco filth on the yard's width you occupy in walking, exhibiting the strangest spectacle of civilized humanity that can well be imagined, a woman claiming good sense, sweeping the streets all about her to make cold and wet her already almost bare feet and ankles!

Nor is this all. These damp winter winds bathe many a bare arm, kiss wantonly many an unprotected neck, and visit rudely many a bosom only vailed with a gossamer gauze. To say nothing of such an exposure to every lewd eye that roves the street, and the unwomanly impudence it offers to every modest gaze, it is a hazardous, wicked, criminal exposure of health, and a total neglect of all the ends and uses of Dress. And then, to crown all, you go out in all weathers with your heads exposed to the fiercest blasts, all unbonneted; for Webster says a bonnet is a *covering* for the head; but few are the women's heads we have seen covered this season—and then wonder why you should have such terrible colds, such troublesome coughs, such griping pleurisies, such burning fevers, and so many ailments!

Now, I ask again, and you shall be judges, young women, if your modes of Dress do not injure your bodies? Do they answer the ends of Dress? Any one who has given the subject a moment's judicious consideration must see that there has been and still is a fearful departure from the real uses of Dress. The primary object of Dress is to clothe and make comfortable the body, so that it may be the peaceful and happy dwelling-place of the spirit in its earthly pilgrimage. But filling it with disease is not making it comfortable. Hampering it in fetters is not making it comfortable.

I have referred to a few of the most prominent evils of our present mode of female Dress. Now, let me ask, if our women would dress warmly and securely from wind and wet, yet not in too close confinement, their feet and limbs; if they would shorten their skirts so they would swing clear of wet, mud, filth, and passing obstacles; diminish their number and dimensions, so that their weight would not be burdensome, and suspend them from the shoulders, instead of girting them around the abdominal and spinal regions; would give their chests a free and easy play; would cover their heads, arms, and necks whenever exposed to cold and damp weather or night air, and would always seek to be clothed easily and comfortably, giving always a sufficiently free circulation of air between their dresses and bodies, to carry off the constant exhalations going out from every living body; if they would thus dress, would they not be far more healthy, happy, and useful? Would the roses not return to their cheeks, the full, swelling beauties of woman's strength to their forms?

This subject has weighty moral and religious considerations connected with it. Have we any moral right thus to abuse our bodies, thus to commit a snail-working suicide? What matters it, so far as the guilt is concerned, whether we kill ourselves in a minute or a year, a year or an age? We have more suicides among us than we sometimes imagine. The young miss goes out in a cold night, with bare arms and head and neck, and wafer-like slippers on her feet, with her waist engirded in cords and whalebones, and her load of burdensome skirts, and dances in high glee two thirds of the night; then, with a vail on her head and her under-garments not yet dry from the recent perspiration, she goes to her cold chamber and bed, to get a troubled sleep, and awaken in a fever which carries her to her grave. Then round her mutilated body gather her mourning friends to bid it a long farewell and hear her minister talk of the inscrutable ways of God's providence. Call it by what name *you* will, to *me* it is suicide. Another, by daily exposures in wet and cold and change of climate in the common woman-dress, takes cold after cold, till a consumption fasters upon her lungs and she slowly passes away. Another circle of mourners weep, and another minister talks of the inscrutable ways of God; but to me it is still another case of suicide. Another passes through the common lot of girlhood, with the common succession of colds and coughs, fevers and pains; in due time marries, with her chest cramped into half its proper dimensions, her lungs small and weak, her female economy all diseased and weakened by the abuses of dress and exposure. At length the period of maternity approaches. Too weak to sustain its labors and burdens, she dies amid them. Friends come weeping again, and the minister condoles them with the sad old story of God's inscrutable ways. But to me it is not inscrutable. It is another case of suicide. Could the grave-yards all over the country speak, they would utter fearful tales of this suicidal abuse of Dress.

The second question is, Do our ideas of Dress corrupt our hearts? One may almost worship at the shrine of Dress. Many are the young ladies whose thoughts rise no higher than the dress they wear and the bonnet that decks their heads. If they can be hung over with gewgaws and tinselry, if plumes shall tremble on their heads, silks shall rustle about them, and jewels shine wherever they go, to catch every eye and bewilder every passer-by, they fancy they are in the upper-ten of womanhood. Vain! The peacock, whose little heart is one beating pulse of vanity, is not half so vain as they. Giddy, trifling, empty, vapid, cold, moonshine women, whose souls can perch on a plume, and whose only ambition is to be a traveling advertisement for the men and women who traffic in what they wear, are many who flaunt in satins and glitter in diamonds. How many such there are we would not say. But I doubt not, that not a little like them are many who are otherwise women. They love Dress; love it inordinately; love it when they ought to love something worthier; and spend their time, and thoughts, and mind, and heart, and money on what they shall wear. The fashion-plate is their profoundest study. The science of dressing is the only one they care to know. The cut of a collar is a matter of sublime importance. How much of this foolish vanity there is in the world! How many otherwise good women does it spoil! And now the question with every young woman should be, How do I feel about my dress? Is it a matter too bright in my eye—a subject too important in my mind? Am I vain of my dress? Does it corrupt my heart, take my attention from virtue, from mental improvement, from the graces of a good life, from religion, from my Saviour, and my God? Do I devote thoughts to Dress that ought to be given to the great problems of duty, life, womanhood, to the development and culture of my powers of heart and mind; to science, conversation, language, and the objects of living? Why am I? Why do I live? To what end? Is there a great object in my being? Have I any thing to do in its attainments? Does my love of Dress interfere with the true objects of woman-life? This is the questioning mind which every young woman should possess. Now let me ask, Does not your love of Dress lead you from the great ends of woman-life? Are you not taken captives by the glitter of Dress? sold bond-slaves to your bonnets and shoes?

Oh, what a fearful waste of time and talent is given to the frivolity and vanity of dress! what a sacrifice of soul and body, principle and life, is made upon its altar!

What multitudes of young women waste all that is precious in life on the finified fooleries of the toilet. How the soul of womanhood is dwarfed and shriveled by such trifles, kept away from the great fields of active thought and love by the gewgaws she hangs on her bonnet! How light must be that thing which will float on the sea of passion—a bubble, a feather, a puff-ball! And yet multitudes of women float there, live there, and call it life. Poor things! Scum on the surface! But there is a truth, young women ; woman was made for a higher purpose, a nobler use, a grander destiny. Her powers are rich and strong; her genius bold and daring. She may walk the fields of thought, achieve the victories of mind, spread around her the testimonials of her worth, and make herself known and felt as man's co-worker and equal in whatsoever exalts mind, embellishes life, or sanctifies humanity.

But notwithstanding Dress has fascinated so many thousands, and led them down the paths of vanity and frivolity, it is still a means of culture, an instrumentality in the hands of virtue, an evidence of civilization. It addresses itself to the taste, and affords opportunity for its improvement. Taste is an element of mind. It is the spring-source of the fine arts, of all the embellishments of life, of poetry, and all that pertains to elegant literature. It is the grand refiner of life. Whatsoever cultivates the taste, develops properly its activities, and refines and elevates its pleasures, does a good office for man. And this is just the proper office of Dress. It is true that Dress has a mission, a good one, a moral one, ay, a religious one. It is a refiner, a cultivator, a subduer of coarseness, barbarity, rudeness. Pity the soul that has no taste for Dress. The Dress of a man speaks out his soul. In other words, a man is known by his Dress; not by its richness, not by its conformity to fashion, but by its neatness, appropriateness, harmony, and the way he carries it. A clown will carry a king's dress clownishly; and a true king will carry a clown's dress kingishly. It is not the Dress that makes the man, but the man that makes the Dress.

Every state of society is manifest in its Dress. The savage is fond of gewgaws, glitter, paint, feathers, colors, mere show, with little or no reference to utility or taste. The barbarian approaches one step nearer the true standard. He exhibits a faint idea of utility and taste; he subdues and blends colors, puts ornaments into use, and varies his Dress a little to suit circumstances. The civilized man shows more taste, less ambition for glowing colors, a greater skill in making, a better idea of fitness and propriety. The enlightened man is more grave in the character of his Dress, wears less ornaments, admits none save where it combines utility and taste, is chaste, subdued, harmonious, classical in every thing that pertains to Dress. We can not yet lay full claims to an enlightened Dress. Our female Dress is a half barbaric costume—a rude mixture of ornament and utility, in which ornament greatly predominates.

Our soldier's Dress, very appropriately, retains all the elements of savagism—high colors, sharp contrasts, profuseness of ornament. This is as it should be. But every enlightened man should regret that our female Dress is not more grave, classical, chaste, subdued, and appropriate, combining taste and utility, refinement and strength. A woman in full street Dress, with her profusion of ornaments, her flounces and fly-about gewgaws, is a very poor representation of good sense, refinement, and cultured, classic taste. If our artists should carve and paint their master-pieces in such taste, we should pronounce it barbarism at once.

I would gladly pursue this theme, and trace the office of Dress in all its operations as a reforming and refining agent, and show how to improve our tastes, correct our judgments, and utilize and at the same time beautify our dresses. But time will not permit. I will only say in addition, that the love of Dress, when properly used, is noble; when abused, is evil; when wisely directed, it combines utility and beauty; when abused, it possesses neither.

But the idea which I am most anxious to impress upon the minds of young women, is the symbolic use of Dress, is the fact that they have *minds* to dress as well as bodies. Our outward Dress should be symbolic of an inward Dress. While we toil to robe in beauty these perishing bodies, we should labor more industriously to adorn those immortal qualities which shall wear their adornments when a new heaven and a new earth shall succeed to those that now are. This is the point at which young women err more than elsewhere. They labor to dress the body, and sadly neglect the soul. O what a fearful dearth of soul-dress, of mental adornment, of interior beauty there is among young women! Scarcely can one in ten of them speak their mother-tongue correctly, converse intelligibly ten minutes upon any subject of common interest, write a simple business or friendly letter correctly, or comprehend the simplest natural sciences. What do they know of mechanics, science, literature, government, theology, history, reform—the great questions that stir the world of mind? How little, how little! There are some noble exceptions to this remark, I know. But we must not disguise the fact, that there is a fearful want of mental culture among young woman. They give forty thoughts to dressing their bodies to one for their minds; they spend forty dollars for bonnets, shoes, and clothes to one for books, instruction, and improvement; they give forty hours to toilet to one to solid study and serious reflection; they put forty adornments upon their persons to one upon their minds. How sad the thought! Compare a well-dressed body with a well-dressed mind. Compare a taste for dress with a taste for knowledge, culture, virtue, and piety. Dress up an ignorant young woman in the "height of fashion;" put on plumes and flowers, diamonds and gewgaws; paint her face and girt up her waist, and I ask you if this side of a painted feathered savage you can find any thing more unpleasant to behold. And yet just such young women we meet by the hundred every day on the street and in all our public places. It is awful to think of. Why is it so? It is only because woman is regarded as a doll to be dressed—a plaything to be petted—a house ornament to exhibit—a thing to be used and kept from crying with a sugar-plum show.

She must learn that she has a great soul, a great mission, a great duty, and a great power, before she will break away from the bonds of the toilet and be herself. Woman by nature is no more a toilet puppet than man. Her mental and moral duties are equal to his. Her powers of mind and heart are equal to his. Her field of labor it is wide as his. Her time is as precious as his. It is as important that her soul should grow as his. She has as mûch need of knowledge, wisdom, courage, strength of mind and purpose, as much need of all the powers and beauties of a cultured soul, as he. Why should she not adorn her mind, develop her powers, live to a high purpose, act well a noble part, do and be according to her capacity? Let young women elevate their aims; give less time to the toilet, more to study, duty, and active employment; regard themselves as something more than dolls, as something intelligent, useful, to be improved, to grow wise and great. Let them dress their minds in wisdom, adorn their hearts with virtue, clothe their souls with strength, with the majesty of noble purposes and high resolutions, and they will soon be something more than automatons on which the milliner and mantuamaker hang their wares.

I have written plainly rather than flatteringly, and I have done so because I believe the time has fully come when woman should be a woman, and not a mere gaudy appendage to man; when her soul should wake up from its long lethargy and put on the habiliments of wisdom and usefulness; when she should live to a grander purpose than she has done, aad should make her power felt more sensibly in the morality and religion, business and bosom, of the world. I am not a disregarder of the beauties and proprieties of Dress. On the contrary, I admire appropriate Dress. It speaks out the man or woman. But I would have everybody feel that the man makes the Dress. Almost any thing looks well on a noble woman. The plainest Dress becomes agreeable when worn by a person of grand purpose and good-doing life. Real life when unadorned is most adorned. Noble womanhood is always beautiful. The world always has and always will admire it. The richest Dress is always worn on the soul. The adornments that will not perish, and that all men most admire, shine from the heart through this life. God has made it our highest, holiest duty to dress the soul he has given us. It is wicked to waste it in frivolity. It is a beautiful, undying, precious thing. If every young woman would think of her soul when she looks in the glass, would hear the cry of her naked mind when she dallies away her precious hours at her toilet, would listen to the sad moaning of her hollow heart, as it wails through her idle, useless life, something would be done for the elevaion of womanhood. I hope I address those who appreciate my words and my feelings. Above almost every thing else do I desire woman's elevation in the moral and intellectual scale of life. You may not see the mental or moral nakedness of the mass of our young women as I do; you may not hear the pleading voice of religion as I do; but I trust you do see your need of higher purposes in life, and more active usefulness; I trust you do see that you have souls to dress and hearts to adorn, and will attend to this, your highest duty.

Lecture Four.

FASHION.

Fashion made Superior to Health—Fashionable Religion—Unfashionable Ministers—Votaries of Fashion Despise it—Fashionable Women Short-lived—Mothers of Great Men Unfashionable—Woman's Greatness shown in Offspring—Example of Women of Fashion—Apostrophe to Fashion—Appeal to American Women—Nature in Freedom's Temple—Fashion is Monotonous—Woman needs more Freedom.

WOMAN IS accused of being the dupe of Fashion. Her fashionable follies are paraded in every public print; her dry-goods propensities are talked of in every circle where she is not truly respected, and in many where she is; her Parisian proclivities are made the butt of very general ridicule, and the dignity of her character is not a little lowered by her too great intimacy with fashion plates and dandy shops. Though, perhaps, man is as much to blame for this as woman—for she seeks to please him, and courts his smiles more than the smiles of all the gods of Fashion—still she must bear her part of the blame—I ought to say guilt—of this terrible and reckless folly.

It is a great fault with American woman, that they worship so blindly at the shrine of Fashion. They sacrifice taste and comfort, time and money, health and happiness, character and life, on this graceless and godless altar, What shopping—what trimming—what sewing and stuffing and padding—what bowing and scraping—what simpering and oiling and scenting—what cooking and spicing and preserving—what eating and sipping and drinking—what wasting and lying and cheating—what gossiping, slandering, and abusing—what forging, straining, and overreaching—what miserable time-serving and eye-serving at the expense of all that is pure and noble in the human heart and life, are resorted to keep pace with the changing moods of Fashion! What is there in our highly civilized life that escapes the palsying touch of Fashion? *Dress*, what is it? Fashion from head to foot. No matter if it outrages all physiology, puts bands around the lungs, gauze on the feet, and hangs multitudinous skirts upon the most vital and yielding portions of the female system. What of all that? Fashion is superior to health and life. What if it shrivel a woman into a mummy, and fade her into a ghost, and plant in her vitals the never-dying worm of consumption! What is beauty and physical womanhood to Fashion? Who would not rather fade at twenty-five, and die at thirty, than to be out of the Fashion?

Food, what is it good for if it is not in Fashion? If it is not greased and peppered, shortened and raised, concentrated and almost distilled, and then taken at hours of *ton*, and in wholesale quantities, of what avail is it? Better have the dyspepsia than eat coarse bread! What woman would not rather have a nervous debility than dispense with hot coffee and strong tea? Then, to refuse roast beef and baked ham would be very ungenteel! A bilious attack would be much more fashionable. It would be unwomanly not to have an animal die every time she was hungry, so that her life might pick the bones of death. It is very poetical to realize that life flowers on the sepulcher of death.

Friendship, its links must be forged on Fashion's anvil, or it is good for nothing. How shocking to be friendly with an unfashionable lady! It will never do. How soon one would lose caste! No matter if her mind is a treasury of gems, and her heart a flower-garden of love, and her life a hymn of grace and praise, it will not do to walk on the streets with her, or intimate to anybody that you know her. No, one's intimate friend must be *à la mode*. Better bow to the shadow of a belle's wing than rest in the bosom of a "strong-minded" woman's love.

And *Love*, too, that must be fashionable. It would be unpardonable to love a plain man whom Fashion could not seduce, whose sense of right dictated his life, a man who does not walk perpendicular in a standing collar, and sport a watch-fob, and twirl a cane. And then to marry him would be death. He would be just as likely to sit down in the kitchen as in the parlor; and might get hold of the woodsaw as often as the guitar; and very likely he would have the baby right up in his arms and feed it and rock it to sleep. A man who will make himself useful about his own home is so exceedingly unfashionable, that it will never do for a lady to marry him. She would lose caste at once.

Religion, too, must be fashionable to be of any worth. What is a church out of Fashion? Who goes there? God never will hear a prayer in such a church, nor pardon a penitent, nor give grace to a striving soul. That antiquated pulpit! Those plain old pews! That queer-looking gallery! Oh, yes; the pews are very comfortable; the singing sounds most admirably; the preaching is God's unvarnished truth quickened by divine love and mercy. Oh, how it would melt one's soul if it was only in a fashionable church. And then the minister. He is such a plain man, and says such plain things; he is all the time talking about such every-day matters, and makes one feel so ashamed because he seems to know just what we have all been doing and thinking about. Instead of preaching about Babylon and Belshazzar, and pouring out his eloquence upon the antediluvians and the glorious company in heaven, he aims every word right at us, and gets so earnest about our daily sins that he really makes one's heart ache. It is unpleasant to listen to such a minister unless one can really forget the world and go with him into his spiritual idea of life. Then he does not try to please the ladies enough. He talks to them just as plainly as to the men. He is always wanting to have them do something that is not pleasant, go to see some poor person, teach some ragged little urchins, give up some fashionable way of life, read some book on duty or some homily on fashionable sins. True, he is a very kind man, the kindest man in all the parish all admit. He never speaks an unpleasant word to any body; it is said he spends half his salary for the poor, and visits them a great deal, and spends much of his time in trying to reform the wicked and dissolute. The common kind of people think he is a great man, and they flock to hear him, and love him strangely. But fashionable people do not go there much, and he gets a poor living. One may know that by his poor dress and small house. So it is; religion must be done up in fashionable order, or it is soon out of date in the market. The minister must be a ladies' man, or the saloon will be more thronged than the church. And to be a ladies' man it is understood that he must be a fashionable man, a conformist, a pliant, time-serving, honey-mouthed, smile-faced, glove-handed, eel-natured kind of a creature, as ready to smile on a sin as a virtue; whose rebukes are so sugared that they are as agreeable to take as homeopathic pills. There are multitudes of churches that have more fashion in them than religion, and enough of worshipers and ministers who think more of the mode than the matter of worship.

Literature must have on it the brand of Fashion, and even education must receive the crown stamp of this graceless monarch, or be rejected by the world and receive no diploma at its hands. It is true that the rule of Fashion is almost omnific. To be out of Fashion is to be a mark for the cold finger of scorn from its votaries, and set up as a target for the shafts of their ridicule. So true is this, that it has become a common saying, that "one may as well be out of the world as out of the Fashion!" Yet what is Fashion, what does it amount to? Is one really more respected, more beloved, more received into the arms of the good, more caressed by the worthy, for being fashionable? We think not. The best and most beloved men and women that have ever lived have been far from the votaries of Fashion. They have lived with little thought and little conformity to the demands of this prince of weak minds. They have rather asked what was right, what was best, than what was fashionable. Conformity to Fashion tends rather to disgust than respect. Deep down in the hearts of all people there is a sense of the hollowness of Fashion, and a just loathing of its pretension and show. Even its votaries secretly despise it, and obey its dictates only because they think they must. They know its baseness better than we can tell them. True, they do not fully realize its sinfulness nor wholly appreciate its evils. But its hollowness and falseness they feel at times most keenly. Else why their perpetual unrest, their longing, dissatisfied condition of mind? Oh, if we could pull off the false glitter that lays like a gorgeous mantle over the fashionable world, we should see such an aching void, such a palpitating heart of woe, as would make the very stones cry out for sympathy. Look at a fashionable woman—one woman, a poor, weak mortal, apprenticed to earth to learn the work of the skies, pupiled here to be schooled in the great lessons of beauty and goodness written on all the outward universe and taught by the constant voice of God in the soul in its best experiences; see such a woman fretting herself well-nigh to death in chasing the butterfly delu sions of Fashion, seeing them fade in her hands as fast as she grasps them, starving her soul and dwarfing her mind in the pursuit of such phantoms, enfeebling her body, irritating her nerves, breaking down her constitution, fading in early womanhood, and dying ere her years are half lived; what object is more sorrowful and has higher claims upon our pity? We think it sad when a woman is thus crushed by neglect or abuse, by the hand of poverty, by hard toil, or the harder fate of a consuming death at the hands of a false or brutal companion. But really, why is it sadder than to die by inches on the guillotine of Fashion? The results are the same in either case. Abused women generally outlive fashionable ones. Crushed and care-worn women see the pampered daughters of Fashion wither and die around them, and wonder why death in kindness does not come to take them away instead. The reason is plain: Fashion kills more women than toil and sorrow. Obedience to Fashion is a greater transgression of the laws of woman's nature, a greater injury to her physical and mental constitution, than the hardships of poverty and neglect. The slave-woman at her tasks will live and grow old and see two or three generations of her mistresses fade and pass away. The washerwoman, with scarce a ray of hope to cheer her in her toils, will live to see her fashionable sisters all die around her. The kitchen-maid is hearty and strong, when her lady has to be nursed like a sick baby. It is a sad truth, that Fashion-pampered women are almost worthless for all the great ends of human life. They have but little force of character; they have still less power of moral will, and quite as little physical energy. They live for no great purpose in life; they accomplish no worthy ends. They are only doll-forms in the hands of milliners and servants, to be dressed and fed to order. They dress nobody; they feed nobody; they instruct nobody; they bless nobody, and save nobody. They write no books; they set no rich examples of virtue and womanly life. If they rear children, servants and nurses do it all, save to conceive and give them birth. And when reared what are they? What do they even amount to, but weaker scions of the old stock? Who ever heard of a fashionable woman's child exhibiting any virtue or power of mind for which it became eminent? Read the biographies of our great and good men and women. Not one of them had a fashionable mother. They nearly all sprung from plain, strong-minded women, who had about as little to do with Fashion as with the changing clouds. I have given considerable attention to this fact. It is worthy of the deepest thoughtfulness. Oh, it is a solemn fact that we descend into our children, in our weakness or strength, in our meanness or majesty, as we have lived. And what a lean, meagre, moonshine inheritance does a fashionable mother convey to her offspring! I confess that to me there is something grand in being the mother of a noble son or daughter, of a strong and virtuous family of children. If there is a just human pride, it may live in such a mother's heart. The mothers of Washington, Adams, and Channing; of Josephine, Hemans, and Stowe, stand higher in my mind than any kings or queens that ever lived. The proof of their greatness was in their children. Such sublime inheritances could not have been given if they had not been possessed. Such grandeur of mind, such greatness of heart, such majesty of soul, such royal worth, are everlasting honors to their noble mothers. And I doubt not but when the vail of flesh is taken from such women, their true greatness will be visible. By the side of such how will stand the fashionable mother? In that upper world, souls will rate according to their real worth, according to the gold that is in them. Oh, if vigorous health, great virtues, a large heart, and capacious powers of mind are to be coveted for any thing, it is that they may descend into our children, and reappear in them, to adorn and bless themselves, us, and the world, and be a glory unto God in earth and heaven. I had rather sire a noble son or daughter than win a thousand victories as brilliant as Napoleon's proudest or sit on the throne of earth's greatest kingdom. To me there is something so grand in virtue, so priceless and deathless, so celestial in the powers of a great and good human soul, that to give existence to one is the cause of a deeper joy and a richer gratitude than is otherwise granted to mortals here below.

In this light, how stands the tawdry foolery of Fashion? and what place does the fashionable woman take?

Then the *example* of a fashionable woman, how low, how vulgar! With her the cut of a collar, the depth of a flounce, the style of a ribbon, is of more importance than the strength of a virtue, the form of a mind, or the style of a life. She consults the fashion-plate oftener than her Bible; she visits the dry-goods shop and the milliner oftener than the church. She speaks of Fashion oftener than of virtue, and follows it closer than she does her Saviour. She can see squalid misery and low-bred vice without a blush or a twinge of the heart; but a plume out of Fashion, or a table set in old style, would shock her into a hysteric fit. Her example! What is it but a breath of poison to the young? had as soon have vice stalking bawdily in the presence of my children, as the graceless form of Fashion. Vice would look haggard and mean at first sight, but Fashion would be gilded into an attractive delusion. Oh, Fashion! how thou art dwarfing the intellect and eating out the heart of our people! Genius is dying on thy luxurious altar. And what a sacrifice! Talent is withering into weakness in thy voluptuous gaze! Virtue gives up the ghost at thy smile. Our youth are chasing after thee as a wanton in disguise. Our young women are the victims of thine all-greedy lust. And still thou art not satisfied, but, like the devouring grave, criest for more. Where shall we get the strong women of the next generation — the women who will live for principle—whose commanding virtues shall be a tower of strength—whose wisdom shall be a poem of prophecy, and whose love a hymn of praise? Who will be the mothers of genius and wisdom, of the manhood and womanhood that shall redeem mankind? Oh, not from thee, all-degenerating Fashion! shall we get them. Thy reign is the blast of womanly virtue and manly strength. Thou art the precursor of destruction. Thou dost intoxicate, bewilder, and make mad the nations whom thou wouldst destroy. Thou dost lead to dazzle and delude to ruin. Avaunt, thou grand sycophant of the nineteenth century, thou vile usurper of the people's throne!

Oh, American women, be exhorted to flee from the sorceress whose enchantments are binding you in the silken chains of an ignoble effeminacy. Your weakness weakens our nation and sends a destructive palsy down into succeeding generations. Your loss of strength is humanity's loss. How can there be individual identity where Fashion rules? how individual taste, individual opinion, individual virtue and character? How can there be genius and talent where Fashion molds the will and cuts the life to a pattern? How can there be wisdom where Fashion dictates the mode of thought and the form of utterance? How can there be greatness where Fashion shapes the growth and prescribes its bounds? There is nothing in our country so paralyzing to the growth of mind and the progress of righteous principles as the easy and general conquest of Fashion over our people. If it were only in matters of dress and equipage, of outward adornment, that it bore sway, it would not be so ruinous. But it goes into every department of thought and life, into opinions, principles, religion. It shapes the creed, prescribes the form of worship, and puts its excommunicating ban upon all heresy. It enters the sweet retreat of home and poisons its love and life. It sets up its proud form in the sanctuary and dishonors worship with its cold formality. Everywhere it is a godless tyrant. To develop our strength of body and mind we want freedom. Genius expands its wings in freedom's airs. Health blooms in freedom's prairie-fields. Wisdom grows in the hermit-cells of individual thought where no binding chains of custom cramp the mental powers. Love is always truest and sweetest and noblest where it is freest. Nature is freedom's temple. No forming shears of Fashion cuts her patterns. She grows every leaf, and opens every flower, and solemnizes every bird-marriage, and utters every hymn of praise in the truthful and innate spontaneity of her universal soul. So humanity should be free; not free to sin with impunity, but free to dress according to its own individual taste and comfort; free to live in homes arranged without respect to Fashion, but agreeable to the wants and interests of their members; free to eat and swear and act as seemeth good in each one's mental sight; free to think and speak on all the great subjects of human interest; to believe and worship by the light of reason and the inspiration of conscience without fear of the guillotine of public opinion established by Fashion. The greatest want of our country is this freedom. We now do every thing so much by rule, that the rule cramps the soul out of every thing done. The rule is always of Fashion's make. We love and marry, educate and worship, by rule. I would not recommend an abjuration of all rules. Rules are good so far as they are just and founded on universal principles. But arbitrary, time-serving rules are evil. In matters of dress I would have every woman consult her own taste, form, complexion, comfort, character, and person. In doing this she may develop her mind, cultivate her taste, and gratify a reasonable desire to please others. Instead of every one's dressing alike as Fashion dictates, let each one consult her convenience and circumstances, and dress as best becomes her ideas of a suitable wardrobe for herself. If one chooses to wear a dress very long, let her do it; another to have her dress Bloomerized, let her do it. If one prefers a close bonnet, another an open; one thin shoes, another thick boots; one a flowing robe, another a tight dress; one a high-necked, another a low-necked dress, one a belted, another a bodiced waist, let it be as each one shall prefer. In a word, let each woman dress herself and her household as her judgment, skill, and taste shall dictate, without everlastingly consulting the last fashion-plate. It would be better that every one was dressed differently from all others, than as now, all rigged up to order by the last nuncio from Paris. In nature, variety spreads a curious interest over all her vestiture. In the human world, Fashion clothes all in a tiresome sameness. To say the least, a very great improvement might be made by a little more freedom and courage, and exercise of individual judgment and taste. As it is, individualism is laid on the shelf, and all are swallowed up in a fashionable generalization. So in matters of household arrangement, in the general character and style of equipage, in food, culinary affairs, social etiquette, and all that pertains to the outward life, to health, to labor, to individual interests, I would have more freedom, ease, and flexibility, would see more of individual judgment and peculiarity, more marks of personal character and affirmative force of will and opinion. As it is, there is a tedious monotony in all these things. Our houses are all made and furnished too nearly alike; and so of all our affairs. A fashionable sameness, somber and dull, spreads over our whole outward life.

Then, in opinions of men and things, of politics and social relations, in education, literature, art, in morality and religion, there should be more freedom, more conformity to individual judgment, more thinking for self and less by proxy, more personal and less party influence. There is a terrible tyranny over us in these things. We are cast in the stiff mold of Fashion. We have our fashionable forms of thought, and seem afraid to break them. We have our formulas and creeds, and they bind us. If there were more freedom there would be less error and atheism. Our minds are all different. No two think exactly alike, or look exactly alike, or feel exactly alike. Then why should we not be free and use our own reason for our own purposes and give others the same privilege? Why be such slavish conformists, and brand as traitors or heretics all who differ from our party or church?

I would awaken young women to these things. They have their individual interests, both temporal and eternal. They have their characters and life-connections to form. They have great and stirring interests to hold in their hands. They have examples to set and lives to live

And they have a mighty influence to exert in their day both upon the present and coming generations, both upon this and the future world. The subject of this essay is one of inexpressible interest to them. Woman is too much in chains. She wants more freedom. And she will never have it till she takes it herself. She should covet and seek a higher life. She should claim her full equality with her brother, man, and strive to show herself worthy. In woman and her life are wrapped up some of the greatest interests and issues of humanity. O that each individual woman could feel it, and live as realizing the solemn fact!

Lecture Five.

EDUCATION.

Life a School—Education a Work of Progress—Schools of Vice—Every Circumstance a Teacher—Kinds of Education—Female Education—True Womanly Ambition—Improve your Opportunities—Principles should be Understood—Time Trifled Away—Some Excuses—Society Needs Woman's Influence—Education as it is—Girls should have Something to Live For

"LIFE is real, life is earnest." To make life grand is the end of living. God has a great purpose in every human soul; that purpose is its *truthful education*. Life is God's school. He is its great superintendent; his Son is prime instructor. The world is His primary school-house, or, rather, our primary school-house built by him. Here we learn the alphabet of things; and learn to spell and read a little from the great book of God. Here we sit in our places and learn our first lessons; stand in our classes and recite them. Here we get ready for that college which God has built for us on the spiritual Mount Zion. In this lower school we prepare for the department above. Our position in that department must be determined by our dutifulness and progress in this. Oh, solemn thought! We must be measured by our merit; we must stand in our lot; "every man in his own order." The deeds done in the body shall tell upon the life of the spirit. What we make for ourselves now, shall be ours in the college-hall above. Wisdom gained in life shall not be lost in death. It will live a halo of brightness, a crown of glory, when "death, the last enemy, shall be destroyed." God did not ask us whether we would come into this primary school or not; whether we would take this lower-world life. Neither will He ask us whether we will go into the higher department; whether we will take the upper-world life. He gave the one; he will give the other. But the *use* we make of these lives He has put not a little into our own hands. What will be in these lives He has left not a little with us. Our standings we are to choose to a certain extent. Our characters are the workmanship of our own hands. Our worth is of our own making. Our *Education* is a personal matter. God has given us minds, a school, a study-room, teachers, all the books of nature, experience, revelation, reason, duty, affection, and now commands us to *educate* ourselves, promising to be with us and assist us as our kind Superintendent in this grand work of life.

Education, strictly speaking, covers the whole area of life. It is the word which means all God asks of us, all we owe to him, the world, and ourselves—that great word which expresses the sum total of human duty. Nor is it confined to this present period of life. To educate is the work of Heaven. Time and eternity are the school periods of intelligence. Reason may have an eternal growth. Conscience may widen its powers and deepen its sanctities in heaven. Affection may grow in beauty and fervor through immortal ages. Mind may expand and intensify through eternity. To educate is to develop mind; to ex pand its capacities; to strengthen its energies; to deepen its affections; to elevate its aspirations; to sharpen its perceptions; to quicken its actions; to intensify its emotions; to harmonize its powers; to empower its will, and magnify its sweep of action.

Education is a work of progress. It begins in life and has no end. Death does not terminate it. We learn the elements of things below. Above we shall study their essences. We progress in proportion to our own efforts. Education may be good or bad, right or wrong. Reason may grow strong in error, may revel in falsities. The will may be mighty for evil. The heart may grow in vice, and the passions expand in misrule. The mind may be educated into terrible confusion, so that its passions will clash in battle array, and its powers war with each other like exterminating demons. The din of mental warfare and the clash of spiritual arms are heard in almost every soul. Terrible conflicts are within us. And whole fields of slaughtered virtues are swept over by their death-dealing siroccos. Like nations of the earth our mental powers are grouped together, and group confronts group like embattled armies, sending their hissing arrows of fiery death into each other's ranks. Power strikes at power, like single combatants on the field of strife. Such is the awful sight seen by God in many a human soul. And such to a greater or less extent is what He sees in each one of us; so direful are the results of bad Education.

Few of us have been educated altogether aright. We have gained much mental strength in wicked conflict. Our passions have expanded in lawless riot. Our mental arms have grown strong in corrupting labors. Our energies have been made vigorous in vicious employments. Our feet have been made active in the dance of folly and the race of mammon. We have risen to power in the service of a tyrant master. We have done the bidding of sin, and made our soldiers broad to bear its Atlas burdens. But Education has made us mighty in evil. Giants in vice stalk about us daily who were sweet and beautiful in their babyhood as ever smiled in a mother's face. On every hand we meet with the graduates of some school of vice, in whom the powers of darkness are mighty for evil. Some come out from the dark holes of intemperance ; some from the luxurious saloons of gambling ; some from the gilded halls of fashion ; some from those dark places where virtue dies a bleeding sacrifice to sensuality. These are the schools in which the mighty in wickedness are educated. And then we have lesser schools all about us in which the young take lessons in vice : schools on the street, schools at home, schools at the toilet, schools in pleasure circles, schools in the market and counting-room, where they take lessons in deception, slander, folly, anger, backbiting, sensuality, and vice. Our schools for Education in evil are numerous, and their teachers are legion. I believe much more in evil Education than in innate depravity. The little cherubs that come into our arms right from the hands of Deity are innocent and pure. The skies above us and the flowers around us are not purer and sweeter than they. Their little souls are immaculate. "Of such is the kingdom of heaven." I can not believe in depraved babyhood; but I must believe in depraved youth and manhood. All about me are the sinful wrecks of once pure souls. It is wrong Education that has made them the sad, pitiable things they are. Oh, what wretched contortions of God's beautiful handiwork have men made of themselves! Of all the things that God has made, the human soul is most perfect and beautiful. The flower and trees and fields are beautiful. The flashing aurora, the golden clouds, the sapphire sky, are beautiful. The circling planets, the blazing sun, the starry canopy, are beautiful. But what are they compared to a human soul? What is an ephemeral flower or an age-lasting star compared with glorious reason, with eternal love, with deathless benevolence, and conscience? What were the material universe with all its sublime grandeur and awe-inspiring magnificence with no soul to gaze upon it? And yet perfect and beautiful as were our souls when God gave them to us, what unsightly, miserable, demoniac things we have made of them! It is evil Education that has done it all. We have trained our minds in wrong schools. We have educated our powers at the feet of evil teachers. We have taken lessons in the science of wickedness. We have followed bad examples and copied corrupt manners. And we still do so. These things have made us what we are.

Our Education is not all got in our organized schools.

Our hired teachers and printed books are not all that act on our powers to develop them. Life is one grand school, and its every circumstance a teacher. Society pours in its influences upon us like the thousand streams that flood the ocean. Scholastic men and women may speak of book Education; it is mine to speak of life Education. Life is my field and my theme; that great common arena where men and women do battle with the forces about them.

We are educating all the time, and the question with us should be, How do we educate ourselves? What manner of men and women do we make of ourselves? The great question of life is an educational one. We all get an Education; but the *kind* is the point for us to determine. Some are educated in vice, some in folly, some in selfishness, some in deception, some in sensuality, some in nothing in particular and every thing in general, some in goodness, some in truth and right, some in theology, and some in religion. Our kinds of Education are legion. We can not live without being educated some way. Every day gives us many lessons in life. Every thought leaves its impression on the mind. Every feeling weaves a garment for the spirit. Every passion plows a furrow into the soul. All is motion in that mysterious, wonder-working house in which we ourselves live—the mind.

Every hour of life has solemn, fearful results. The question should hang all the time written in blazing capitals in the firmament of each soul, "How am I educating?" It is wicked to let the crazy world educate us as it will.

It is awfully hazardous to yield ourselves up, as most people do, to the circumstances of society about us. It is a fearful risk to plunge into the stream of popular custom and float on like a dead sponge drinking in its turbid water. Most people are like mocking-birds and monkeys, repeating all they hear and mimicking all they see. Our duty is to educate ourselves as we should.

Having hinted these general principles of Education, we may now address ourselves especially to young women, and apply them to their life. The daily life-education of the mass of young women is not what it should be. It is much like the life-education of the mass of young men. It is the Education of circumstances, custom, society, etc. Young women live, think, and act just as society dictates. They wear what fashion says shall be worn; they say what etiquette say is proper; they do what custom dictates; their ideas of gracefulness, propriety, and life are molded in the common mint of popular sentiment. They float on the stream of society mere automatons in the great hand of the world. They do not direct their own Education as though they had any object in life. They seem to lay helpless in the hands of the world, the pets or playthings of the day. These remarks are not very inapplicable to young men also. There is a great body of young men who float on the stream of life with no self-direction. Ask one of them what he lives for, and he will tell you, "to chew tobacco, swear, be a man;" and his idea of being a man is to be able to do these things with grace and dignity. To ask any one of the mass of young women what she lives for, and if you can get her to say it out, she will tell you, "to get married." Now it is certainly right to get married, and to live with this object in view. But there is a grand educational preparation needed for this. And this preparation is the very thing most neglected. Every young woman should have some noble purpose in life, some grand aim, grand in its character. She should, in the first place, know what she is, what powers she possesses, what influences are to go out from her, what position in life she was designed to fill, what duties are resting upon her, what is she capable of being, what fields of profit and pleasure are open to her, how much joy and satisfaction she may find in a true life of womanly activity. When she has duly considered these things, she should then form the high purpose of being a true woman, and of making every circumstance bend to her will for the accomplishment of this noble purpose. There is no higher thing beneath the bending heavens than a true woman. There is no nobler attainment this side of the spirit-land than lofty womanhood. There is no purer ambition than that which craves this crown for her mortal brow. To be a genuine woman, full of womanly instincts and power, possessing the intuitive genius of her penetrating soul and the subduing authority of her gentle, yet resolute will, is to be a peer of earth's highest intelligence. All young women have this noble prize before them. They may all put on the glorious crown of womanhood. They may make their lives grand in womanly virtue. There is in every woman-child the seed of womanhood. She may water and nourish that seed till it shall blossom in her soul and make her spiritually beautiful. Woman has a power, a woman-power, something peculiarly her own in her moral influences, which, when duly developed, makes her queen over a wide realm of spirit. This she can not exert only as her powers are cultivated. It is cultivated woman that wields the scepter of authority among men. Wherever cultivated woman dwells, there is refinement, intellectual and moral power, life in its highest form. To be a cultivated woman, one must commence early and make this the grand aim of her life. Whether she work or play, travel or remain at home, converse with friends or study books, gaze at flowers or toil in the kitchen, visit the pleasure party or the sanctuary of God, she should keep her object before her mind and tax all her powers for its attainment. She must learn to make the most of opportunities. One fault with our young women is, that opportunities avail them but little. They see much and perceive but little, talk much and think but little, hear much and learn but little, read much and acquire but little.

I suppose almost every young woman has seen many steamboats, yet it may be doubtful whether one understands the mechanical principle by which they are propelled and directed. They have seen the flowers and vegetation, birds and beasts, of our region of country, and yet they doubtless are about as ignorant of them as of the products of the torrid zone. They live under our form of government, yet how many know wherein it differs from other governments! They have heard or read of almost every science, yet how little acquainted are they with the commonest principles of science! They have all had their countenances daguerreotyped, yet who knows how it is done? They all wear silk, cotton, linen, yet who knows the history of either one of these articles of apparel? They have bodies "fearfully and wonderfully made," yet how little they know of their structure, laws, and uses! They have minds, beautiful and immortal gifts of divine wisdom and goodness, yet how little attention have they given to learn their principles of action! All around them are little worlds of every-day things upon which they have never bestowed a passing thought, things which are full of interest; yet the common habit of seeing much and thinking little has led them into this same superficial habit. It is like the young man of whom I was told a few days since, who had traveled all over the world, rode on every sea and ocean, and visited every principal seaport, and yet knew nothing of any of them. It is a sad fault with us all, and especially with women—we don't *think* enough. The mass of young women trifle a great portion of their life away on the smallest imaginable things. They chatter like birds and gabble like geese, without the trouble of *thinking*. The things they see and hear every day awaken no consecutive thought. The stars shine above them, and they call them pretty things, but never ask the astronomic story of their magnificence. The world beats its great march of life around them, but they seek not to know the rich lessons of human activity therein. I know that society does not hold out so great inducements for woman to think and educate herself as it ought. I know woman is oppressed with legal and customic disabilities. I know she is shut out from many fields of activity and industry for which she is eminently fitted by her natural endowments. I know that her labor is not half rewarded, that her ambition is cramped into a narrow field. I know that by custom and law she is the slave of man, who holds her person, children, and property in his custody. I know that men think they must be silly and simpering in woman's presence, because they suppose she can appreciate and enjoy nothing higher. I know that many men have an awful horror of "strong-minded women," really educated women. I know that any thing beyond housewifery or parlor gracefulness by many is considered unwomanly; yet woman may overcome all the obstacles in her way if she will educate herself to *think*, and think soundly and forcibly. She must be her own deliverer from these barbaric customs and laws, and her own *thought* must be the instrument of delivery. Let women everywhere become solid thinkers so far as their capacities will admit, instead of triflers; let their life-education be deep, useful, and practical, instead of superficial and theoretical; let them be as well acquainted with the principles of society as they are with those of fashion; let them be as much interested in human progress as they are in dress and gossip; let them take into their hands the keys of knowledge and unlock the storehouses of practical wisdom all about them, and go in and lay hold of the treasures, and human society would soon blossom as the rose. The great thing needed now by our society is more woman-influence—more woman-thought, character, and power. Our female Education is too superficial, trifling, babyish. Our girls are not half developed. Our young women do not exhibit one half their real strength and beauty. Their minds are robbed of much of their natural vigor. They are dwarfed by their delicate nutriment.

As soon as a little girl begins to be a young lady she must be shut up in the house; talked to as though she did not know much; read novels; be dressed up; go to parties; have suitors; take lessons in music; have a dancing master; visit the theater; go a term or two to the young ladies' seminary to practice calisthenics; study Botany without seeing a flower, Astronomy without looking at a star or planet, Geology without stepping into the dirt or putting her hand upon a rock; write a half-dozen compositions on friendship, mother, and home; daub a little in water-paints; receive a diploma, and then set up for matrimony. This is female Education—without an object, without ambition, without point or force, without strength, depth, or breadth. It is simply a little outside polish. It does not teach how to *think;* it does not develop mind; it does not confer power; it does not form character; it does not fix the will, direct the life, establish opinion, deepen sentiment, or do any thing to make a true woman.

Our young women want a more vigorous, practical, and useful Education, one that shall develop strength, character and resolution; one that shall give growth to the mind, power to the will, and efficiency to the life; one that shall enable any woman to be independent, true to herself, to entertain and maintain her own opinions, to get her own living, to mark out her own course in life, to count one in any position she may choose to occupy, to be all that may belong to a free, independent, accountable, intelligent creature. They want to be educated so they will know their own powers, understand their own duties, and comprehend the value of life too well to waste it on trifles. They want to be able to *know* the world in which they move, to take an active part in all life's duties, to converse intelligently upon all ordinary subjects, and make a useful figure in the circles in which they move.

Woman's powers are eminently practical. She has a strong judgment, a rich store of practical good sense, an ample fund of tact, skill, shrewdness, inventiveness, and management. Women are the best managers in the world so far as they have had experience and a field of action. Not one whit behind are they in every department of life to which they have had access.

Now if our girls were reared to the practical duties of life, trained to some great and good end, taught to live for something, have some grand and noble purpose in life, and live to that purpose, how much richer in all that embellishes life and magnifies humanity would be our world!

Our boys have something to live for. Each one says, "I'll be this or that; I'll do so and so when I'm a man. The world must know that I live. I must hew out my way, make me a mark, tell a story that my fellows shall hear." And so each one educates himself into his purpose. But how is it with our girls? What do they live for? What do they expect to be and do when they are women? They have powers equal to the boys—can play as well, run as fast, learn as readily, manage as skillfully, perceive as quickly, are as dutiful, useful, and efficient. Why should the boys grow up with a great and good purpose before them, while the girls grow up for nothing? See what a woman has to do, and what mighty springs of action and influence she holds in her hands. She sits on a throne of power at the very fountain of life. She is goddess of all the springs and little rivulets of humanity. She makes men and trains them. As mother, wife, and friend she wields a triune scepter of vast power. She rears the twigs that grow into the oaks of the world. She may bend them at her will. If woman was rightly educated, who could tell what a race of men would grow up to people the coming ages? How can the woman-mind, undeveloped, untrained, uninspired with great aims, grand and brave resolutions and actions, impress the minds of the generation to come with strength, power, activity, intellectual and moral vigor? It can not. Oh, it is a burning shame that our women are not educated to a greater vigor of body and mind! They should be strong in will thought, action, love, resolution. They should be stout-hearted, high-souled, brave-purposed, yet always womanly. If the world were mine, and I could educate but one sex, it should be the girls. I could make a greater and better world of the next generation by educating the girls of this. It is not half so important that our legislators be wise, as that our mothers be so. It is not half so important that our men be brave, as that our women be so. Strengthen the women-heart, and you strengthen the world. Give me a nation of noble women, and I will give you a noble nation. Cultivate the woman-mind if you would cultivate the race.

Lecture Six.

PHYSICAL AND INTELLECTUAL DEVELOPMENT.

Natural Position of Woman—Relations of Body and Mind—Sound Minds only in Sound Bodies—To be Healthy is a Duty—Physical Laws Obligatory—Penalties for Violation—Girls and their Grandmothers—Causes of Difference—Physiological Studies Advised—Women the 'Weaker Vessel;' Why?—Intelligence and Beauty—Woman's Sound Judgment—Woman's Mind not Powerless—Finished Educations—Education at Home—Schools only Helps to Education—Woman's Thought Wanted.

We have treated the subject of education in its widest and most general sense. We propose now to treat the same general subject more definitely in relation to *Physical and Intellectual Development.*

Such is the natural position of woman in human society, that the welfare and progress of that society depends in no small degree upon her culture. She presides over the fountains of life, all life—both male and female. She impregnates every human being with the qualities of her soul. She images herself in all men's being. Into the very woof of existence she weaves the shreds of her own being. Woman's soul colors, forms, molds, modifies, endows the soul of humanity. It is so. It must be so. The infant-mind sleeps in the mother-mind till all its powers are set and their tendencies established. The child-being is subject to every mood of mind and state of body which exists in the mother-being. Then the early twig is nurtured and the early blossom unfolded on woman's bosom. Woman performs the first work of culture, imparts the first ideas, awakens the first thoughts, aspirations, and emotions, stirs the first tides of feeling, and wields the first scepter in the minds of all men. In a secondary sense, she is the maker of all men. This being the primary fact of human existence, her education is the first work in human progress. To cultivate her is to cultivate the race. To elevate and dignify her is to elevate and dignify the world. As she goes up she bears every thing human with her. Depress her, and the world sinks. If you would ennoble and dignify the world, do this for its women, and the work is done. If you legislate for the world, legislate for woman. If you would educate the world, educate woman. If you would give freedom to the world, give it to woman. If you would redeem the world, redeem woman. The world lies in her arms. She nurtures it on her bosom; she rocks it in her cradle; she breathes into it the breath of its mental life. Above her it can not rise. She is the fountain, and the stream rises not above it. What woman is in any nation or age, the people of that nation or age will be. Noble women give nobility to the sphere of action and influence in which they move. Genius, worth, mental and moral power, owe more to woman than to all things else. If I wished to bless the world, I should bless woman. If I wished to sweeten a stream, I should mingle the sweet in its fountain. If I wished to make an oak strong, I would put water and nourishment at its roots. If I wished to rear me a noble horse, I should take care that its mother possessed the strength and qualities I wished in the animal. It is clear to my mind, if we would do a good thing for mankind, we must do it for woman. Woman should be unshackled, her soul set free, her ambition awakened, her nobility developed, her strength nurtured, her mind educated, her normal sense quickened, her consciences sanctified, her affections taught to wind their tendrils about all that is noble.

Such being the natural position of woman, we hold it as a self-evident truth, that she should be educated deeply, thoroughly, solidly; that the first work of every reformer, every philanthropist, every statesman, every Christian, is to help and urge onward the education of woman.

I. The dwelling-place of the human mind, the instrument of its actions in its world-sphere, is the body. Between the mind and body there is an intimate, mysterious, and wonderful relation. They act and react upon each other. The condition of each one affects the condition of the other: a diseased body tends to produce a diseased condition of mind; a disturbed mind wears upon the body; a nervous hot-blooded body is a constant irritation and flame to the mind; a passionate, restless mind gives no peace to the body.

Thus they act and react upon each other in all their multiform movements, conditions, and activities. No action or condition of the one is negative to the other. The state of the body, then, is important to the mind, to its free and easy action, to its natural growth and ready culture. This is a fact criminally overlooked by the great mass of mankind, and especially by women. It is overlooked by many teachers, and in our general system of mental education.

To train the body is our first care. To develop its strength, to secure and preserve proper tone, to make it harmonious, active, and beautiful, to plant in its vitality the roses of health and sow in its blood the seeds of enduring life and activity, is our first and imperious duty. To neglect the body is to neglect the mind. To abuse the body is to abuse the mind. To enervate, irritate, or corrupt the body is to produce a like effect upon the mind. To beat, bruise, and shatter the house in which we live is to do violence to the dweller therein. Every pain in the body. every weakness, every injury done to it, does a harm to the mind. In ordinary life we do not receive this as true; yet in all severe cases we know it is so. But there can be no doubt that it is true the world over and life through. The mind is our principal care. And we are to nurture our bodies as the present instrument of mental action. If the instrument is shattered and diseased, the action of the mind will be correspondingly imperfect and weak. The body is the instrument on which the mind makes the music of life; and if we would have that music harmonious and sweet, we must have a good instrument and keep it in good tune. The wonderful genius of Ole Bull, whose strains seem almost divine, and full of the mysterious and infinite depths of meaning that belong to music in its highest power, could never make the notes of woe or joy dance at his will like things of life, from the strings of a broke and rickety instrument. He must have an instrument alive in every nerve, sound in every limb, perfect in every part, sensitive to the touch of the sounding bow, before his genius can revel in the melody of music and charm the souls of others in the ecstasies of musical delight. So it is with our bodies. They must be perfect in all their wonderfully and fearfully made parts before the minds which use them can make harmonious the music of life. This is no idle dream. It is the language of philosophy, the utterings of experience, the voice of reason. A sickly body will never do well the biddings of the mind.

It is so; it must be so; virtue can never be all she may be and ought to be, in a sickly and fevered body. Reason can never wield her grandest scepter of power on a shattered and trembling throne, Love can never be that pure, constant, heavenly flame which is a proper symbol of divine affection in a bosom racked with pain or oppressed with weakness. The divine energies of humanity can never urge the soul to a realization of its highest ideals of excellency in a frame overcome with disease, relaxed with dissipation, or oppressed with unnatural burdens. Yes, the body must be sound, healthy, perfect, to realize the highest mental states of which we are capable. Feeble and sickly is the best culture we can give to a mind locked in a feeble and tormented body. No proposition is clearer then, than that we should nurture, cherish, and invigorate our bodies with the most watchful care and rigid and healthful discipline. It is wicked to neglect or abuse them. We violate the most sacred principles of duty when we harm the dwelling-places of our souls. To carelessly expose ourselves to any physical danger, to engage in any species of dissipation or intemperance, to ruthlessly waste in any way the physical energies which God has given us, to recklessly weaken, sicken, mar, or injure our bodies is as much a sin as to violatate the commands of the Decalogue, or deny in practice the principles of the moral law. God will not hold such an offender guiltless. The visitation of His retribution is and will be upon such transgressors. It is our duty to be healthy, to obey the physical laws of our being, to possess sound and active bodies. Every pain, fever, sickness, is a retributive evidence of a violation of these laws; and for every such violation we not only suffer physical evil, but we suffer mentally, morally, socially, and spiritually. We belittle ourselves in the sight of God and men, bemean ourselves in the presence of the moral law, and stay more or less our progress in the great educational work of life. If we would be eminently pious, benevolent, and good, we must be healthy. If we would be endowed with wisdom, virtue, and love, we must be healthy. If we would win men's deepest confidence and God's highest approval, we must be healthy. If we would develop most vigorously all our powers of mind and heart, and give the richest possible culture to our souls, we must be sound in body. If we would impart the greatest possible intellectual and moral vigor to the generation to come, we must obey the laws of health. If we would progress most rapidly in the divine life, and win the brightest laurels for our spiritual brows, we must cultivate well our physical powers. Life's attainments and heaven's joys are not a little affected by our physical conditions. We are of those who believe that we have no right to abuse our bodies, no right to be the puny, feeble, sickly things the most of us are; no right to carry about consuming disease and cankering maladies that eat out our joys and waste our powers. We have no right to make our bodies pestiferous hospitals to bear about the seeds of disease, weakness, and misery. Our physical education is the very first thing to be attended to. In childhood and youth it is a matter of great moment. Every child should be thoroughly instructed in his physical duties, and every youth should make himself wise in all matters pertaining to life and health. I deem this subject of vast importance to young women. Their usefulness and happiness depend in no small degree upon it. Their progress in the arts of life, their influence on the generations to come, their degree of culture and power, depend much upon their obedience to the laws of health. If they would be the women they ought to be, noble, high-minded, matronly women, impressed with a lofty sense of their duty and high and generous conceptions of womanhood, it is imperatively important that they cultivate judiciously the greatest possible strength and activity of body. What a sickly womanhood grows up in a nervous, feeble, neuralgic, splenetic female body!

How is it with our young women? Are they vigorous and healthy? Can they eat well, sleep well, work well, walk well, bear well the changes of climate, endure heat and cold, toil and fatigue, trial and study? Are their forms full of life and health, their muscles full of strength and activity, their chests well expanded, their lungs full and free, their hearts large and strong, sending out the currents of life ladened with their stores of well-formed nutriment? Ah, would it were so! But we know it is not. Our young women are sickly house-plants, that a chill wind will shake or an untimely frost nip and wither. They are pet-birds, with no strength of wing to bear life's long, brave flight. Colds and coughs, aches and pains, weaknesses and diseases innumerable prey upon them. They faint at the sight of a spider and scream at the far-off hiss of a serpent. They are full of weaknesses and pains that wear out life and enervate all their mental and spiritual powers. The women of our day grow old in their youth. They often have all the marks of fifty years of age at twenty-five—decayed teeth, sallow skins, sunken cheeks, wrinkled faces, nervous debility, and a whole crowd of female ailments. Our grandmothers at sixty years were stouter and more capable of endurance than our young women at twenty-five. Why is it so? Simply because our girls and their mothers have neglected to cultivate their physical powers. They have been shut up in tight rooms, bound up in bandages, fed on sweetmeats and spices, doctored with poisons, dressed in whalebones and death-cords, petted like house-plants, steeped in tea and coffee, till they are nothing but bundles of shattered nerves and diseased muscles. There may be noble exceptions, but this is the general rule. Our men and women are all too weak and sickly. But we know that our men are by far the most healthy. And well it may be so. Our boys are turned out to stretch their limbs and try their muscles, while the girls are compelled to look at them through the windows. It is a burning shame to imprison all the little girls in the country, to shut them in from the fresh air and the life-giving sun, from the green fields and the flowing water-brooks, from the woods and hills where health is breathing in every gale and strength is made at every bounding step. All the girls should wear good, tight boots, loose, flowing short-dresses, open sun-bonnets, and then run, and shout, and laugh in natural out-of-doors glee. They should sleep in cool, well-ventilated rooms ; eat simple, coarse, plain food ; exercise much in health-giving work and play; drink pure, cold water, and bathe in it daily ; be taught to practice temperate, prudent, and regular habits ; learn the laws of health and how to obey them, the physiology of their own bodies, and what is demanded for health and strength. Such a course of early physical training will impart beauty, vivacity, cheerfulness, amiability, strength of mind, warmth of heart, and moral stability, more surely and rapidly than can otherwise be done. Girls thus trained will possess a higher and nobler womanhood, exert a wider and deeper influence in their families and spheres, impart firmer bodies and richer minds to their children than those who are rocked through girlhood in luxury and dress and shut up in confined air and more confined dresses. We are pampering our women to death. We are killing them with tenderness, not with enlightened moral and affectionate tenderness, but with the tenderness of folly, fashion, luxury, idleness, with the tenderness of vicious habits of life.

My advice to all young women is, that they learn the laws of health and strength as soon as possible, and obey them to the very best of their ability; that they study the physiology of their own systems, and know how fearfully and wonderfully they are made, and what conditions of life are necessary to the fullest and most perfect physical development; that they live with the resolute determination that they will be well, and that not a pain or weakness shall be felt without tracing it immediately to its real cause and applying the proper remedy at once; that health shall be deemed a condition of happiness and its maintenance a religious duty; that sickness shall be considered a sin and pain, a just chastisement of God for it. When our young women are thus physically trained, they will be prepared to bless the world as it never has been blessed; they will usher in a period of moral and intellectual grandeur such as the world has never witnessed; they will exert a strong woman-influence in every sphere of thought and action which will be at once refining, ennobling, and redeeming; they will so establish correct habits of living, so sanctify the altars of home, so adorn the walks of social life, that the very heart of the great body of society will throb anew with fresh impulse of life and send out its currents of health and strength to the remotest parts.

II. With such a physical preparation, we are ready for intellectual action, for the education of mind.

Woman has not had a fair chance for the culture of her mind. She has been continually anathematized and tormented with the idea that she is the "weaker vessel." Her father, her brother, and her husband have always told her that her mind was weak and small, and that it could not comprehend great things nor do great works. Sometimes her mother and sister are joined in this wholesale slander of the female mind. When a little girl she has been paralyzed with the thought of her inferiority. All through her youth it has been a dead weight on her mental activity. Through her life it has ever muffled the harp of her heart and weighed down the wings of her aspirations. It has been an incubus of discouragement in all intellectual pursuits. How could woman be any thing with the whole world against her? with even those she loved best, and in whose judgment she most confided, all the time reminding her of her mental weakness and inferiority? And as it has been, so it is. Woman is still believed intellectually inferior to man, by ninety-nine one hundredths of mankind. Poor, weak, silly, drunken, half-idiotic men, whose wives have to support them, will tell you in conscious pride of sex of woman's weakness of mind. I have heard little Lilliputian men, whose minds were as small as a baby's rattle-box, always harping on this worn-out string of woman's weakness of mind. It is an idea not peculiar to enlightened people. The savages believe it, and many of them believe that she is only a pretty beast without a soul that is given to man to bear his burdens. Among savage, barbarous, and half-civilized people, woman's inferiority is never questioned. The idea is entertained in its bald usurpation and black injustice without a questioning thought. Among us it is covered over a little with cotton beauty and rolled up in sugar-plum sweetness so the woman will bear it a little better. Our women are tickled with the idea that they are the *beauty*. Our public speakers, lecturers, papers, speak of the audiences of *intelligence* and *beauty*, meaning by *intelligence* the men and by *beauty* the women; a deep insult to the woman-mind.

I freely admit that the mass of men in our country do possess more intelligence than the women; but the reason is not because of woman's inferiority, but because of her oppression and want of opportunity. She has not had half a chance. She has been shut out from almost every field of intellectual labor, barred from every position of trust and profit, laughed at by baby men and silly women if she attempted to devote her life to intellectual pursuits, opposed with the most barbarous legal disabilities and the still more barbarous incubus of public opinion. Yet notwithstanding all this oppression and want of opportunity, she has shown a quickness of perception, an intuitive acumen, a sharpness of forecast and solidity of judgment that among nearly all married men has made her opinion a matter of great importance. Few are the married men that are willing to risk a disrespect of their wives' judgment in any important matter. An eminent lawyer of Virginia once told me that but twice in his married life had he acted counter to his wife's advice, and in both instances his judgment failed and hers was right. Many men have found their wives' intuitive judgment so correct that they dare not resist it, as though it were the utterings of an oracle. It is well known that such men as Bonaparte and Jackson have relied with great confidence upon their wives' opinions. So universal is this opinion among men, that all our best moralists and most sage philosophers advise all married men to consult their wives on all important matters, and to be very cautious about resisting the settled convictions of woman, not as a matter of courtesy or policy, but because of the accurate perceptions and sound judgments of woman's mind.

This is not all fustian for the flattery of women; it is the deliberate conviction of our best and wisest minds. And yet a great majority of these same minds can not get rid of the idea that woman's intellect is inferior.

Though the mass of women of all countries have been intellectually undeveloped, we have instances enough to show that the woman-mind is as powerful, close-sighted, and active as man's. Women have ruled the mightiest nations, mastered the abstruse sciences, led vigorous armies to victory, written powerful books, made vigorous and brilliant achievements in eloquence, commanded vessels, conducted complicated commercial relations, edited influential journals and papers, sat in chairs of learning and done every thing necessary to show that the female mind is not wanting in power. Yet if the female mind were weaker, it is not an argument against its education. Mind should be educated, whether little or much, weak or strong. And woman's natural position is such, that all the mind she has should be developed and richly cultivated.

We talk much about female education; we have female schools and colleges; and one might think, to read of them, that we educated the female mind. But it is a sad mistake. The greater part of our female seminaries and colleges are mere shams. They do not develop mind. They do not train its muscles to hard work; they do not discipline its nerves to close application and vigorous research; they do not harden its hands to the toil of thinking, nor strengthen its arms to battle with the intricacies of science nor the problems of metaphysics. They are mere gilding shops, whitewashing establishments, paint factories, where girls are polished to order with the etiquette of boarding-school finish.

We send our girls to these schools to be educated; but educated for what? Why, nothing in particular; but to be educated because it is fashionable; to go home and sit in the parlor *educated ladies;* to talk about novels and poetry with the gentlemen that come in; to go into ecstasies over some boy's *last;* to set up for a professional husband. It is to go *over*, not *through*, some of the sciences, but do it because it is fashionable; recite and write and go through all the forms of school training, just because it sounds well and will give a lady social position, not literary standing or scientific character, intellectual influence, or dignity of thought and life ; and go through it all and graduate with diploma in hand at fourteen or sixteen years of age. Here again women are cheated with a bauble. Little girls are told that they are educated at this tender age, and to prove it are referred to their diplomas, announcing to the world that they have been through a regular course of study at such an institution. Only think of it—a finished education at sixteen! Why, the majority of our young men can not get ready for college till they are twenty or twenty-five. There they spend four years in hard study and the most vigorous mental discipline, delving in the deep mines of science and untombing the rich archives of history and human thought; then study three years the masters of their professions. And even then they are but boys in thought and action, and must meet the hard discipline of active life before we award to them intellectual manhood. We compare these educated girls with these educated young men, and wonder at the weakness of the female mind! The girls went to school because it was fashionable; the boys at the call of an honorable ambition. The girls studied to appear well in society; the boys to tread life's highway with honor and win laurels from the hand of the world in the duties of useful professions. The girls were stimulated by nothing that was great and noble in action; the boys were fired by all that can stir up human ambition. True, the innate glory of cultivated minds was before them both, but that alone in our present sensuous life has seldom been found a sufficient stimulus to vigorous intellectual discipline. I should be glad to see a class of our strongest young women go through Dartmouth, Yale, and Cambridge colleges with the same preparation and stimulants that our young men possess. If I mistake not, they would graduate with honors, and be heard from in the high field of intellectual life.

But as this can not be at present, our young women must make the best of the opportunities they have. What education they do get should be thorough, practical, and from proper motives. They must fill woman's place, and they ought to prepare for it as thoroughly as possible. They have an intellectual life to live and intellectual duties to perform. How poorly they will live that life and perform those duties without a preparation. Many young women can not attend school and enjoy the common routine of mental discipline; but they may read and study at home; they may cultivate their minds by the fireside; in the lecture-room, in the church, and in the intellectual circle. The midnight hour may impart strength to their minds, and the morning dawn may find them storing them with useful knowledge. The world is full of good books, and from them they may glean invaluable treasures. Every young woman spends time enough in idle gossip and foolish flirtation to educate herself well. Schools are not necessary — they are only helps to education. Many great minds have been educated without them. To educate is to learn to think. The way to learn to think is to practice thinking "Practice makes perfect." The archer practices with his bow; the artist with his brush or chisel; the writer with his pen; the mechanic with his tool; the lawyer with his brief. So the student should practice with his mind—practice thinking, reasoning, investigating, analyzing, comparing, and illustrating. This is the practice our young female minds want. They do not think enough. They do not dig for thought, search for ideas, investigate for truth. They are too light, frivolous, and giddy. They will run by a great thought to trifle with a silly whim. They will leave a rich intellectual lecture for a giddy party. They will turn away from a mental feast to enjoy an idle gossip; I mean too many of them will.

How beautiful, how truly captivating, is an intellectual woman! We have many such among us, and their number is increasing. The female mind is awakening from its long slumber. In ten years we shall have many more. Our present female education will soon be too superficial. These surface students will soon be left in the shade. Woman is hearing the voice of God which commands her to use well her talents. Soon He will call for them, and she must answer for their use. It is an omen of good that woman is rising and putting on her strength. She has a rich mind, and I am glad that she is becoming aware of it.

Young women, heed the voice which asks you to educate. If you heed it not, you may look meagre and antiquated by-and-by. In that "good time coming" how sad a thing will be an uneducated woman, one whose mind is barren of thought! You are to live, or ought to live, through two generations. If you live only for to-day, you will be minus to-morrow. If you live for to-morrow, you will be bright lights in your day and generation. There is a work for you to do. You must sanctify the thought of the world. Our men are too worldly and sensual in their intellectuality. You are to redeem their minds from this baseness. We want more pure thought, more sanctified mind, more looking upward toward goodness, heaven, and God. And with your assistance we may be redeemed from this downward tendency. I have often said it: the world wants more woman's thought. It is too masculine, hard, inflexible. Our men think too much by rules of logic. Educated women would be more intuitive, spontaneous, religious. You may remedy this evil. Much responsibility rests upon the young women of to-day. Let them know it, and lay aside their folly and lightness and put on the garments of wisdom and truth.

Lecture Seven.

MORAL AND SOCIAL CULTURE.

Woman Judges by Impressions—Mental Powers should Harmonize—Effects of Different Culture—Male and Female Minds Differ—The Female Mind Analyzed—Feminine Purity—Woman's Benevolence—The Sentiment of Duty—Integrity in Woman—Cultivate Regard for Truth—Piety the Crown of Moral Virtues—Cultivation of Piety Urged—Development of Social Nature—Friendship and Love.

FEW subjects can be more interesting to high-minded young women than those which are the theme of this Lecture—MORAL and SOCIAL Culture. Concerning the moral and social deportment of women's nature there can be no difference of opinion. I am happy in knowing that although men differ about woman's intellectual capacities, they agree in ascribing to her the highest order of moral and social qualities. All admit that woman is the morality and religion, the love and sociality, of humanity. In these developments of human attainments, she is the queen without a peer. These are at present woman's peculiar fields of power. Society has measurably shut her out from the intellectual arena of life. But if it has cut short her operations in this, it has extended them in the field of social life. Wide and grand are her opportunities here.

Man is not so deficient in gallantry as he is in generosity and judgment. In what man has oppressed woman, it is more the fault of his head than his heart; it is more a weakness of conscience than of affection. He is prouder of his judgment than he ought to be. His judgment often fails because it is not sanctified by conscience. His intellect is often deceived because its vision is not extended and widened by a deep affection and a broad benevolence. In this, woman has the advantage of him in the present relations of the sexes. Her moral sense consecrates her intellect, and her heart quickens it, thus making her judgment more intuitive and ready, more comprehensive and sure. She *feels* that a thing is so; he *reasons* that it is so. She judges by *impression* when facts are stated; he by *logic*. Her impressions she can not always explain, because her intellect has not been sufficiently cultivated; his logic often fails him, because it is not sufficiently imbued with the moral element. The light of the conscience and the heart does not shine upon it with sufficient strength. This we understand to be the present difference between the male and female mind. It is more than a difference in growth and culture, in inherent constitution. We do not believe that the relation between the different departments of the human mind naturally differ in men and women; that is, we do not believe that man is more intelligent and less moral, and women more moral and less intellectual. A perfect male mind is an equal strength of the several departments of mind; that is, an equal strength of the intellectual, moral, social, and energetic portions of the mind, a balance among its several powers. The same is true of the female mind.

So far as this relation of the parts is concerned, it is the same in the perfect male and female mind. In just so much as this relation is changed, is the judgment corrupted and the mental strength impaired. In the present male mind this relation is changed by giving the greater cultivation to the intellect, and less to the moral sense and the heart. So his judgment is impaired and the moral dignity of his soul debased. He is a less man than he ought to be ; is deformed in his mental growth, like a tree grown in a shady place where the light could reach it from only one quarter. He has less power of mind than he would have with the same amount of cultivation properly and equally distributed among the several departments of his mind. Strength lies in balance of power. Our men are not too intellectual, but too intellectual for their moral and affectionate strength. They are like an apple grown on all one side, or a horse with disproportioned body, or any animal with some of its limbs too short for the rest. Mentally they are deformed and lame by their one-sided culture. In the present female mind there is a disproportion in another direction. In this the intellect has been neglected, while the moral and social mind has had a better degree of cultivation. Thus our women have been mentally deformed and weakened. They are less woman than they ought to have been. Their characters and judgments have lacked harmony, and their lives have been marked by the same deficiencies.

Their minds are one-sided, and marked with sad irregularities. They are not too moral and affectionate, but are not sufficiently intellectual. The same amount of culture which they have received would have conferred more beauty and dignity to the character and life had it been more general, or equally applied to the several powers of mind. Sound judgment, pure life, dignity of character are the results of a balance of power and culture in the several departments of mind. This difference in the culture of the male and female mind has made a breach between the sexes. The present male mind can not comprehend the female, nor the female the male. Instead of growing up in similarity and harmony, they have grown up into wide differences.

Our present men and women are not in harmony with each other. There are cultivated antagonisms of mind between them. They can not see, feel, nor think alike. Their lives are impregnated with a different spirit. And this is one of the primary and fruitful sources of unhappiness in the marriage relation. Men and women are so different in their cultivation that they are not in their natural harmony. Our men are not natural men, nor our women natural women. The nature of each is warped by culture, and warped in different directions.

The male and female mind are not alike by nature, by any means. There is a wide difference between them; but the difference is in the nature, texture, and quality of the mind, and not in the relation of parts. The female mind has an inherent constitution peculiar to itself that makes it female ; so with the male. This difference is beyond the fathoming line of human thought. We know it exists, but wherefore and how we know not. It is the secret of the Divine Constructor of mentality. In our mental structure we are to seek for harmony, a consistent rhythmic development of parts. The opportunities offered to woman for the cultivation of her moral and religious nature are eminently favorable. If her intellectual opportunities are not so good, her moral and religious are better. She is not so pressed with temptation. The world does not bear with such an Atlas burden on her conscience. The almighty dollar does not eclipse so large a field of her mental vision. Material pursuits do not check so much her spiritual progress. God is nearer to her heart, more in her thoughts, sweeter in her soul, brighter in her visions, because she is less compassed about by the snares of vice and the hostile pursuits of the false and flattering world. It is a blessed thing for humanity that woman is more religious and morally upright; because man is too irreverent and base. He lacks the sanctity of high morality and the consecration of religion. I speak of man in the mass. Woman is the conservation of morality and religion. Her moral worth holds man in some restraint and preserves his ways from becoming inhumanly corrupt. Mighty is the power of woman in this respect. Every virtue in woman's heart has its influence on the world. Some men feel it. A brother, husband, friend, or son is touched by its sunshine. Its mild beneficence is not lost. A virtuous woman in the seclusion of her home, breathing the sweet influence of virtue into the hearts and lives of its beloved ones, is an evangel of goodness to the world. She is one of the pillars of the eternal kingdom of right. She is a star shining in the moral firmament. She is a princess administering at the fountains of life. Every prayer she breathes is answered to a greater or less extent in the hearts and lives of those she loves. Her piety is an altar-fire where religion acquires strength to go out on its merciful mission. We can not over-estimate the utility and power of woman's moral and religious character. The world would go to ruin without it. With all our ministers and churches, and bibles and sermons, man would be a prodigal without the restraint of woman's virtue and the consecration of her religion. Woman first lays her hand on our young powers. She plants the first seeds. She makes the first impressions; and all along through life she scatters the good seed of the kingdom, and sprinkles the dews of her piety. But woman does not do enough. Her power is not yet equal to its need. Her virtue is not mighty enough. Her religion comes short in its work. Look out and see the world—a grand Pandora's box of wickedness—a great battle-field of clashing passions and warring interests—a far-spread scene of sensualism and selfishness, in which woman herself acts a conspicuous part. Look at society—the rich eating up the poor; the poor stabbing at the rich; fashion playing in the halls of gilded sensualism; folly dancing to the tune of ignorant mirth; intemperance gloating over its roast beef, or whisky-jug, brandy punch, champagne bottle, bearing thousands upon thousands down to the grave of ignominy, sensualism, and drunkenness. Is there not a need of more vigorous virtue in woman? Is there not a call for a more active religion, a more powerful impulse in behalf of morality? Who shall heed this cry of wicked, wasting humanity, if young woman does not? To youthful woman we must look for a powerful leader in the cause of morality and religion. The girls of to-day are to be greatly instrumental in giving a moral complexion to the society of to-morrow. It is important that they should fix high this standard of virtue. They ought to lay well their foundations of religion. They ought early to baptize their souls in the consecrated waters of truth and right.

I. The first element in their moral character which they should seek to establish firmly is *purity*. A pure heart is the fountain of life. "The pure in heart shall see God." Not only is purity of life needed to make a young woman beautiful and useful, but purity in thought, feeling, emotion, and motive. All within us that lies open to the gaze of God should be pure. A young woman should be in heart what she seems to be in life. Her words should correspond with her thoughts. The smile of her face should be the smile of her heart. The light of her eye should be the light of her soul. She should abhor deception; she should loathe intrigue; she should have a deep disgust of duplicity. Her life should be the outspoken language of her mind, the eloquent poem of her soul speaking in rhythmic beauties the intrinsic merit of inward purity. Purity antecedes all spiritual attainments and progress. It is the first and fundamental virtue in a good character; it is the letter A in the moral alphabet; it is the first step in the spiritual life; it is the Alpha of the eternal state of soul which has no Omega. Whatever may be our mental attainments or social qualities, we are nothing without purity; only "tinkling cymbals." Our love is stained, our benevolence corrupted, our piety a pretense which God will not accept. An impure young woman is an awful sight. She outrages all just ideas of womankind, all proper conceptions of spiritual beauty. To have evil imaginings, corrupt longings, or deceitful propensities ought to startle any young woman. To feel a disposition to sensuality, a craving for the glitter of a worldly life, or a selfish ambition for unmerited distinction is dangerous in the extreme. It is the exuding of impure waters from the heart. Who feels such utterings within should beware. They are the whisperings of an evil spirit, the temptations to sin and crime. If I could speak to all the young women in the world, I would strive to utter the intrinsic beauties and essential qualities of purity; I would seek to illustrate it as the fountain of all that is great and good, all that is spiritually grand and redeeming. There is no virtue, no spiritual life, no moral beauty, no glory of soul, nor dignity of character without purity.

To be pure is to be truthful, child-hearted, innocent of criminal desire or thought, averse to wrong, in love with right, in harmony with whatsoever is beautiful, good, and true. This state of the soul is subject to cultivation. It may be made strong and active. By personal effort, by constant watchfulness and striving, every young woman may be pure ; but she need not expect to be without. She must watch, and strive, and pray if she would be pure. If she does not, she will become corrupt before she is aware of it. The world will send into her heart its putrid streams of influence to corrupt and debase it.

The second virtue she should cultivate is *benevolence.* Queen of virtues, lovely star in the crown of life, bright and glorious image of Him who is love, how beautiful is it in woman's heart! A woman without benevolence is not a woman; she is only a deformed personality of womanhood. In every heart there are many tendencies to selfishness, but the spirit of benevolence counteracts them all. A hollow, cold, graceless, ungodly thing is a heart without benevolence. In a world like this, where we are all so needy and dependent, where our interests are so interlocked, where our lives and hearts overlap each other, and often grow together, we can not live without a good degree of benevolence. Our true earth-life is a benevolent one. Our highest interests are in the path of benevolence. We do most for ourselves when we do most for others. "It is more blessed to give than to receive." Good deeds double in the doing, and the larger half comes back to the doer. The most benevolent soul lives nearest to God. A large heart of charity is a noble thing. Selfishness is the root of evil; benevolence is its cure. In no heart is benevolence more beautiful than in youthful woman's. In no heart is selfishness more ugly. To do good is noble ; to be good is nobler. This should be the aim of all young women. The poor and needy should occupy a large place in their hearts. The sick and suffering should move upon their sympathies. The sinful and criminal should awaken their deepest pity. The oppressed and down-trodden should find a large place in their compassion. How blessed is woman on errands of mercy! How sweet are her soothing words to the disconsolate! How consoling her tears of sympathy to the mourning! How fresh her spirit of hope to the discouraged! How soft her hand to the sick! How balmy the breath of her love to the oppressed! Woman appears in one of her loveliest aspects when she appears as the practical follower of Him who "went about doing good." The young woman who does these works of practical benevolence is educating her moral powers in the school of earnest and glorious life. She is laying the foundations for a noble and useful womanhood. She is planting the seeds of a charity that will grow to bless and save the suffering of our fellow-men. In no other way can she so successfully cultivate the virtue of benevolence. It is not enough that she pity the sorrows of the poor and suffering. Her hand must be taught to heed the pleadings of her pitying heart. What she feels, she must do. What she wishes, she must make an effort to accomplish. What she prays for, she must strive to attain. Everybody predicts a beautiful life from a good-doing young woman.

Active and cheerful should be every young woman's

efforts for the needy. Thus will she make to herself a large heart of benevolence, and draw around her a large circle of admiring and worthy friends.

The third virtue which the young woman should cultivate is *integrity, or the sentiment of duty.* A German philosopher has poetically and truthfully said, "The two most beautiful things in the universe are the starry heavens above our heads and the sentiment of duty in the human soul." Few objects are richer for the contemplation of a truly high-minded man than a young woman who lives, acts, speaks, and exerts her powers from an enlightened conviction of duty; in whose soul the voice of duty is the voice of God. In such women there is a mighty force of moral power. Though they may be gentle as the lamb, or retiring and modest in their demeanor, there is in them what commands respect, what enforces esteem. They are the strong women. The sun is not truer to his course than they to theirs. They are reliable as the everlasting rocks. Every day finds in them the same beautiful, steady, moral firmness. Men look to them with a confidence that knows no doubt. They are fearless and brave; they have but to know their duty to be ready to engage in it. Though men laugh or sneer, though the world frown or threaten, they will do it. There is no bravado in them; it is the simple power of integrity. They are true to what to them seems right. Such spirits are often the mildest and meekest we have. They are sweet as the flower, while they are firm as the rock. We know them by their lives. They are consistent, simple-hearted, uniform, and truthful. The word on the tongue is the exact speech of the heart. The expression they wear is the spirit they bear. Their parlor demeanor is their kitchen and closet manner. Their courtesy abroad is their politeness at home. Their confiding converse is such as the world may hear and respect them the more for it. Such are the women of integrity. Men love to trust their fortunes in their hands. The good love to gather around them for the blessing of their smiles; they strew thei pathway with moral light. They bless without effort; they teach sentiments of duty and honesty in every act of their lives. Such is the rectitude of character which every young woman should cultivate. Nothing will more surely secure confidence and esteem. There is especial need of such cultivation, for young women are doubted in many respects more generally than any other class of people. Most people seldom think of believing many things they hear from the lips of young women, so little is genuine integrity cultivated among them. I am sorry to make such a remark. I wish truth did not compel it.

I would that young women would cultivate the strictes regard for truth in all things; in small as well as in im portant matters. Exaggeration or false coloring is as much a violation of integrity as a direct falsehood. Equivocation is often falsehood. Deception in all forms is opposed to integrity. Mock manners, pretended emotions, affectation, policy plans to secure attention and respect are all sheer falsehoods, and in the end injure her who is guilty of them. Respect and affection are the outgrowth of confidence. She who secures the firmest confidence will secure the most respect and love. No love is lasting but that which rests in confidence. Confidence can only be secured by integrity. The young woman with a high sense of duty will always secure confidence, and having this, she will secure respect, affection, and influence.

The fourth virtue of inestimable value which the young woman should cultivate is *piety*. This may be regarded as the crown of all moral virtues. It is that which sanctifies the rest. It is a heavenly sun in the moral firmament, shedding a divine luster through the soul—a balmy, hallowing light, sweeter than earth can give. Piety is the meek-eyed maid of heaven, that holds her sister Faith in one hand and Hope in the other, and looks upward with a confiding smile, saying, "My treasure is above." Of all the influences wrought in the human soul, the work of piety is the most harmonizing and divine. It subdues the flesh and the world, and calls down Heaven to bless the happy pietist. It is the constant, ever-speaking voice of the Father uttering in sublime and beautiful impressions the holy eloquence of his everlasting love. It is the communing ground of the mortal child with the immortal Parent. In the mind of youthful woman it is as beautiful as it can be anywhere. And when she consecrates all her powers by the laying on of its heavenly hands, and sanctifies all her feelings by its hallowed influences, she exhibits a view of beauty—of physical, moral, and spiritual beauty—not elsewhere surpassed on earth. A deep, pervading, all-controlling piety is the highest attainment of man on earth. It is that reverent, humble, grateful, affectionate, and virtuous purity of spirit in which the human and divine meet and embrace each other. It is the spiritual crown which men put on when they go into the kingdom of heaven. This is what we urge as the last and finishing excellency of the youthful female character. The cultivation of this is what we press as conferring mortal perfection of character, or as great perfection as frail, sinful creatures can put on below " the mansions of the skies."

We urge it as the best and highest duty of every young woman—a duty she owes to herself, her fellows, and her God—a duty as full of joys as the heavens are of stars, and when performed, reflecting matchless grace upon her soul. We do not urge it through fear of hell or hope of heaven; we do not urge it from motives of policy; we urge it for its own intrinsic worth; for the blessedness of being pious; for the excellency and worth of character and life it confers. No character is complete till it is swayed and elevated by genuine piety. No heart is fully happy till it is imbued with the spirit of piety. No life is all it may and should be till its motives are baptized in the waters of piety. No soul is saved till it is transformed by the gracious spirit of this daughter of the skies. This divine grace of the soul should be sought by every young woman, and cultivated with the most assiduous care, for without it she is destitute of the highest beauty and divinest charm and power of womanhood.

II. Thus cultured and growing morally, the young woman should not forget to develop her social nature by the hand of prudent culture. She is made to love; not only to love one being, but all her fellows. Around kindred spirits should be linked the chain of friendship, and this chain should be kept bright by gentle and confiding usage. Nothing is more proper than that young women should learn how to choose friends wisely. Friendship and love are blind impulses. They need a guardian and guide. Discretion should be that guide. It is natural for us to love what is lovely; but as to what is lovely we often differ. What is lovely to one is not always lovely to another. But there are qualities of mind and heart that are intrinsically lovely, and about which there can be no difference of opinion. What is virtuous, good, amiable, high-minded, generous, self-sacrificing and pure, we all admire. What goes to make a perfect character, a moralist, a Christian, a wise man or woman, is agreeable to us all. Now this is what we should love. This is what we should seek in our friends. It is not a beautiful person, or bland and polite manners, or any thing that belongs to the exterior being that we should love. It is inward worth and beauty—loveliness of spirit. Around the soul should be woven the cords of friendship and love. The outward is deceitful and perishing. The inward is true and lasting. Our affections should be taught to fix themselves on the inward. Where we see inward beauty, there we should fix the seal of our friendship. And our affections should be taught to conform to this rule. No matter how attractive the outward person, if inward attractions, such as worth, wisdom, weight of character are wanting, we should not be moved to love. The one grand rule is to let worth of mind, beauty of soul, fix our affections in the social intercourse of life. Young women can not be too particular in obeying this rule. Their moral and spiritual life, their value in the world, their well-being and happiness depend upon it. If their affections are not brought to act wisely, to cling to the good and the true of soul, they will yield them untold misery. If they love the good, the high of soul and large of heart, they will be happy, inexpressibly happy in the action of their affections.

Lecture Eight.

EMPLOYMENT.

Employment a Duty—Powers Developed by Labor—All Females are not Women —Dependence usually Ignoble—Adversity gives Strength—Girls should have Trades—Self-reliance necessary to Women—Do Something and Be Something —Riches no Excuse for Idleness—Employment gives Activity and Strength—Labor considered Vulgar—Life is given for Employment—Woman was Made for Usefulness.

I TAKE it that men and women were made for business, for activity, for employment. Activity is the life of us all. To do and to bear is the duty of life. We know that Employment makes the man in a very great measure. A man with no Employment, nothing to do, is scarcely a man. The secret of making men is to put them to work, and keep them at it. It is not study, not instruction, not careful moral training, not good parents, nor good society that makes men. These are means; but back of these lies the grand molding influence of men's life. It is Employment. A man's business does more to make him than every thing else. It hardens his muscles, strengthens his body, quickens his blood, sharpens his mind, corrects his judgment, wakes up his inventive genius, puts his wits to work, starts him on the race of life, arouses his ambition, makes him feel that he is a man and must fill a man's shoes, do a man's work, bear a man's part in life, and show himself a man in that part. No man feels himself a man who is not doing a man's business. A man without Employment is not a man. He does not prove by his works that he is a man. He can not act a man's part. A hundred and fifty pounds of bone and muscle is not a man. A good cranium full of brains is not a man. The bone and muscle and brain must know how to act a man's part, do a man's work, think a man's thoughts, mark out a man's path, and bear a man's weight of character and duty before they constitute a man. A man is a body and soul in action. A statue if well dressed may *appear* to be a man; so may a human being. But to *be* a man and *appear* to be are two very different things. Human beings *grow*; men are *made*. The being that grows to the stature of a man is not a man till he is made one. The grand instrumentality of man-making is Employment. The world has long since learned that men can not be made without Employment. Hence it sets its boys to work—gives them trades, callings, professions—puts the instruments of man-making into their hands and tells them to work out their manhood. And the most of them do it somehow; not always very well. The men who fail to make themselves a respectable manhood are the boys who are put to no business, the young men who have nothing to do, the male beings that have no Employment. We have them about us—walking nuisances—pestilential gas-bags—fetid air-bubbles, who burst and are gone. Our men of wealth and character, of worth and power, have been early bound to some useful Employment. Many of them were unfortunate orphan boys, whom want compelled to work for bread—the children of penury and lowly birth. In their early boyhood they buckled on the armor of labor, took upon their little shoulders heavy burdens, assumed responsibilities, met fierce circumstances, contended with sharp opposition, chose the ruggedest paths of Employment because they yielded the best remuneration, and braved the storms of toil till they won great victories for themselves and stood before the world in the beauty and majesty of noble manhood. This is the way men are made. There is no other way. Their powers are developed in the field of Employment.

Men are not born; they are made. Genius, worth, power of mind are more made than born. Genius born may grovel in the dust; genius made will mount to the skies. Our great and good men that stand along the paths of history bright and shining lights are witnesses of these truths. They stand there as everlasting pleaders for Employment. Now what is true of men in this respect is equally true of women. If Employment is the instrumentality in making men, it is equally so in making women. A human female is not a woman till she makes herself so. There is something noble, glorious, in a woman. She is the impersonation of spiritual beauty. But all females are not women. There are scores of them who are only female humanities; and scores more who are only *ladies.* A lady and a woman are two very different things. One is made at the hands of fashion; the other is the handiwork of God through the instrumentality of useful Employment. A lady is a parlor ornament, a walking show-gallery, a mistress of tongue-tied etiquette. A woman is a consecrated intelligence—a love baptized—a hand employed in the work of good. To be a woman requires exertion and prudence. Women are not born; neither do they grow up of themselves; they are made. Their virtues blossom in the garden of industry. Their fruits ripen on the boughs of toil. Their treasures grow on the tree of labor. A woman with nothing to do can not develop a truthful womanhood. A woman with no Employment for her hands or mind can be only the shadow of a woman. What is noble in her will doff its nobility. What is strong will become weak, and she will soon be an imbecile dependent on some one else.

A dependent life is an ignoble one, unless compelled by misfortune; just as ignoble in woman as in man. No woman of health and sound mind should allow herself to be or feel dependent on any body for her living. The sick are always dependent, though they have wealth at their command. But the well should never be dependent. To eat and wear the fruits of another's labor, tends to degradation. To feel that one is shining in borrowed plumes and eating the bread of dependence, is degrading to a noble mind. A noble mind will not willingly do it. The want of Employment, and the dependence of many women, have ruined their characters and made them little else than nuisances to their fellow-men. Thousands of women have no Employment, and live through life in a state of abject dependence. What are they, what can they be, under such circumstances? It requires Employment to develop men, why should not it to develop women? Dependent men are ninnies, why should not dependent women be? Where is the difference between the male and female mind, that one should be expected to be noble and magnanimous under circumstances which would be ruinous to the other? We know that a young man thrown upon his own resources is more likely to be a great, good man than when cradled upon the lap of luxury or fortune. Why is it? Simply because he seeks Employment and depends upon himself for what he is to be and do. He leans not on another, and hence grows strong by standing alone. Plant an acorn in the crevice of a barren rock, and it will strike down its roots and send them out in search of fastening places till it will surround the rock with a net of clinging fibers; and as the winds grow fiercer and the storms howl wilder, the oak will strike deeper and wider its anchoring roots. It will brace itself to meet the emergencies of its life. It will nerve its energies to stand its ground. It will gather vigor from every storm, resolution from every wind, strength from every defiant bolt from heaven.

So it is with man. Place him on his feet in a hard place, where the suns of life strike hotly upon him, and the storms blow fiercely, where he must stand by his own strength or fall, and he will grow into strength by the very pressure of adverse circumstances. Every blow of his own will give it strength; every effort of his mind will give it vigor; every trial of his character will knit firmer its binding fibers. This is equally true of woman. Her character is formed and her power developed in a similar way. A woman can no more be a true woman than a man can be a true man without Employment and self-reliance. I would have every boy and girl in the whole country taught to make their own living at some useful Employment; to mark out for themselves a sphere of action and then fill that sphere; to be useful in some honorable pursuit. I would not put the boys to trades and professions to make them great and good, and fold up the girls' hands and lay them away in the drawer or shut them up in the parlor. I would not make the boys self-reliant and vigorous by generous Employment, and the girls weak, puny, and dependent by idleness or folly. I would not give the boys opportunities to develop their powers and become noble men, and deprive the girls of all these glorious privileges. I would not open a thousand avenues to distinction, wealth, and worth to the boys and comparatively none to the girls. I would not send the boys out into the field of life bravely to earn their own living, and grow strong in doing it, and the girls out to beg their living of the boys, and grow weak and worthless in their dependent beggary. I like the girls too well to have them thus mistreated. I would give them just as good a chance as the boys have. They should not be degraded with half-pay, and only two or three ways to get a living, just because they were made to be women. They should not be shut out from a thousand avenues of distinction and usefulness, for they are richly endowed, just because they are made to be women. They should not be made to feel that it is degrading to be a woman, to feel, as a man expressed it to me the other day, that "women are such good-for-nothing creatures." I love noble, "strong-minded," and strong-hearted women. I wish we had more of them. I know of no way to make them but to give our girls more active Employment. Every girl should have a trade, a business, a profession, or some honorable and useful way of gaining a livelihood—some Employment in which her powers of body and mind may be amply developed. If she has not, she will be dependent upon somebody, and her dependence will degrade her; and her want of Employment will keep her a half-developed specimen of humanity.

If I had half-a-dozen boys, and should let them grow up in play around my house and on the streets, in visiting, gossiping, dressing, riding, dancing, asking nothing of them only to bring me my slippers, or some occasional act of kindness now and then, my neighbors would all cry out against me, declaring that I was spoiling my boys. They would denounce my course as absolute unkindness to the boys; would declare that they never would be any thing with such a miserable training. And yet my neighbors treat their girls in just this way. Now if it will spoil the boys, why will it not spoil the girls? If it is unkindness to the boys, why is it not unkindness to the girls? If boys can not be any thing with such a training, how can the girls be?

If the present generation of boys should be reared just as we are rearing our girls, what a puny race of men we should have with which to commence the next century! Men complain that women are such weak, good-for-nothing creatures that they are only fit to be wives and mothers. Now it seems to me that no woman is fit to be a wife and mother until she is a strong, self-reliant woman, both bodily and mentally. I take it that the more vigorous a woman's body and mind are, the better she is qualified to fulfill the duties of wife and mother.

I take it that the more self-reliant and independent a woman is, the better she is qualified to be a helpmate for her husband, and a wise and judicious counselor for her children. I take it that dignity of character, power of action, resolute will, commanding judgment, steady temper of mind, strong inward resources, are as essential in a good wife and mother as in a good husband and father. In a word, I take it that all that is noble, dignified, useful, and beautiful in character and life, is as essential in women as in men. If so, then why not give woman opportunities such as are necessary to develop her powers and form her character? Those opportunities can not be given without Employment. We can not make men without Employment; how can we expect to make women? How can a woman who has no aim in life, who lives to no purpose, who has nothing to accomplish, whose hands are idle, whose mind has nothing on which to fix its energies—who, in a word, spends a listless, trifling life—how can such a woman possess weight of character, force of mind, or mental worth? When God calls for her stewardship, how can she answer with any honor to herself? When she comes to see her soul disrobed of mortality, how naked and undeveloped it will look!

It appears to me that every young woman should aim to be something and do something. Her powers of mind and body should be applied to a good end. Her hands should be set to some useful employment and made skillful in it. It matters not so much what it is, as how she perseveres in it.

Great men are made in all trades and professions. So may great women be. Woman may rightfully employ her powers wherever she may do it most successfully to herself and her fellows. If our young women feel that they can sell tape and pins, set type or make shoes, keep books or manage a telegraph office; if they can keep a bakery or a drygoods store, direct a daguerreian gallery, or do any thing else that is right and proper to be done, let them not hesitate to do it. Let them accomplish themselves in the art or business that to them seems most agreeable, and set up for themselves. They will be a thousand times more happy and useful than in leading listless and thriftless lives. The kind of Employment is not a matter of so much importance as the fact of being employed. Our boys choose their occupations; so should our girls. But they should always choose to do something that is useful. Our homes are full of necessary and useful employments. Our girls should engage in them with zeal.

No matter if they are rich. They need Employment

just as much. A rich young man is not excused from business—from acting nobly his part in life, and doing something worthy of a man. And if he excuses himself he will only be despised by the community in which he lives. We all understand that a young man has got a part to act in useful life, whether he is rich or poor. Why should it not be so with a young woman? Why should we excuse her on account of her riches? Why should she excuse herself? Idleness is the ruin of her body and mind; Employment will give both activity and strength. She will be wiser, better, happier by being employed in something that will benefit herself and the world. We have a strange theory about our young women that are well to do in the world. We think that they must be great babies, and be fed, and clothed, and housed, and posted about in carriages, waited upon and petted as though they were made for nothing else. It is horridly vulgar for such young women to work. It would be a violation of propriety for them to be useful. They would lose caste if they should engage in any useful employment. So they must be useless appendages, hung about the body of humanity to torment themselves and as many others as they can. What a torment it must be to them to lead such aimless lives, studying all the while for some new way to kill time! How many women there are over whose heads time drags heavily! They have nothing to do The dull round of society is irksome. They have stood at the toilet till every thing there is fatiguing. They have talked over and over their little round of fashionable nonsense. They are weary of their monotonous, inactive, inglorious life. Thousands are the women in easy circumstances who feel thus. They would be glad to lift up their hands and do something, but the chains of custom and fashion are upon them. A false social position has made them timid and fearful. I know that many noble women are weary of such a life. They are tired of being dolls. They would be glad to be women and fill the places of useful, energetic, resolute women.

The position of dependence in which society places its wealthy and easy circumstanced women is directly calculated to destroy their self-reliance and force of character. They are attended by servants wherever they go, who do what they ought to do, and often think what they ought to think. The woman who always asks her servant to do what she may do herself, soon becomes dependent upon and loses a good portion of herself in her servant. If my servant eats my dinner for me, he gets the benefit and I lose it. If my servant takes my morning bath from me, he gets the benefit and I lose it. If he takes my morning walk for me, he receives what I lose. So if he takes my Employment, does what I may and ought to do myself for my own good, he receives the benefit while I lose it. Thus it is that this system of servitude in all its forms tends to degrade the party to whom the service is done. To have done for us what it is best we should do ourselves always injures us. If we have duties to perform, and hire or command another to perform them, we rob ourselves of one of the richest blessings that can come to a mortal being—the consciousness of having performed a duty and the improvement gained by its performance. Thousands of women in our country are greatly injured by the presence of their servants. Servants do for them what they ought to do for themselves. They acquire the habit of dependence, and it soon degenerates them into petty tyrants. If I had but two lessons to impress upon the young women of my generation, the first should be that a useful Employment is the primary means of developing a true womanhood.

I know there is an antipathy to labor among a large class of women; I know that women as well as men seek to avoid care and responsibility; I know that useful Employments are looked upon as hard necessities, to be avoided if possible. But still I know that Employment—daily, constant, responsible Employment—is the stepping-stone to mental and moral worth, to usefulness and happiness. I do not contend for degrading toil, but for honorable, mind-developing, soul-redeeming, heart-adorning Employment. Both men and women are made better by useful Employment. Life is given for Employment; our powers are made for activity. If God had intended that any of us should be idle, he would have built houses, made clothes, cooked victuals, formed characters, accumulated knowledge, and had every thing that we need both for mind and body ready made at our hands. But not so. He has made all that is grand in life, that is glorious in thought, depend upon our own exertions. This is as true of women as of men. Then the idler is a leech on himself—his own despoiler. An idle woman is as base a thing as an idle man. She was made for usefulness. A drone in any hive is a base bee—a nuisance, a leech, a moth.

I know young women have refined ideas of delicacy; sometimes imagine it is vulgar to be useful; that delicate hands are evidences of ladyship. They ought to know that a delicate hand is an evidence of a shallow brain; that a soft hand is an evidence of a soft head. Ladyship and womanhood are two things. A soft hand and a faint heart may make one, but not the other. Womanhood is put on by industry in the pursuit of good. It is made in the field of noble Employment.

I seek to elevate woman. I look to her elevation as the elevation of the race. I see in her powers capable of great actions and a sublime life; but I see no way in which those powers can be developed and that life lived but in active and useful Employment. Woman ought to stand by man's side in all that is great and good in thought and action. The history of every country should have as much to record of woman as of man; but this can never be until woman's field of Employment is extended. She must go out and work. She must do her own business, execute her own intentions, act nobly her part in life wherever she can be the best rewarded for her industry and judgment. I would not make woman unwomanly, but would crown her with all the grace and dignity of true female worth. I look to useful Employment as the best and only means of securing this end. Idleness will not make any woman womanly. Ignorance of business and the world will not. In the pursuit of their own elevation let them learn how to be true to themselves and their duties, and we shall soon have a generation of women such as the world has never seen—of strong, brave, accomplished, and useful women whom history will record as the benefactors of their race.

Lecture Nine.

HOME.

Maternal Love—Ideas of Future Home Universal—Heaven's Home Perfected—Home the Garden of Virtue—Home Influence Permanent—Home is Woman's World—Place does not constitute Home—Our Homes will be like us—Home a Sensitive Place—Home Habits Second Nature.

My theme is *Home*. If my essay could be as good as my subject it would be worthy of devoutest attention. I believe that there are three things of universal interest among men—*Mother, Home, and Heaven.* In all ages and countries mother has been a sacred word. It has laid on the heart of childhood like a dew-drop on the rose, sweetening and refreshing it. A man loves to think of his mother; of her watchful care, her tender vigils, her holy charity, her forgiving goodness, her matchless and marvellous love.

What a great refreshing fountain of life is a mother's love! We all turn to it as the heart's common resting-place. We love to think of our mothers. They loved us with such a deep devotion; did, and sacrificed, and suffered so much for us; were so unselfish and ready to forgive, so vividly alive to our interests, and felt their beings so intertwined with ours that we feel that we must love them. It is the last and lowest ingratitude of a human heart not to love its mother. God made the mother. Such love is Heaven's work. Not in angels' hearts beats a sweeter, deeper, richer feeling. Mother is another name for consecrated love. Not all the theologians in the world could convince me that the natural mother-heart is not holy. I have seen too deeply into my own mother's soul; I have felt too much of the fire of her deathless love; I have witnessed too many evidences of its immaculate purity to believe it inherently depraved. I have always felt that it was a slander against our own mother to believe the mother-heart naturally corrupt. Yes, all the mother is holy. God loves the mother for what she is. She is a reflection of himself. The gates of his everlasting Home will never close against a mother. Though she may be wicked in other respects, in her maternal heart lives a germ of the tree of life which can never wholly die. What love sometimes beams in a wicked mother's heart! All mothers are alike. The wise and the foolish, the idiotic and philosophic, the rich and poor, the cultivated and barbaric, are all the same in love; the same beautiful, tender, forgiving spirit of devoted affection dwells in all. Oh, see the mother as she gazes fondly upon her child; as she feeds him from her breast; as she watches by his sick couch; as she counsels him to virtue and goodness; as she weeps over his waywardness and toils for his happiness!

All the arching glory of the moral world bows in reverence before the mother's love. This is the radiant center, the focus of human affection. And this is the central sun of *Home!* Home has no permanent force, no abiding stability without a mother's love. Take mother out of Home, and the Home is gone. She is the regulator, the mainspring, the center around which all else revolves. How rich is every Home that has in it a true mother! If there were no other attraction in this sacred spot, no other charm, the mother's presence would make it dear and glorious. While a mother lives, Home will be a blessed place. Then *heaven* is another word of universal use and power. In every human soul there lies an idea of heaven; dim and shadowy sometimes, bright and glorious at others; but yet everywhere present. The Arab wanderers, the wild men of the forest, the jabbering Ajetas, the South Sea Islanders, the wall-girt Chinamen, the sable Ethiopians, the cultured Christians, all cherish the thought of heaven —another home, a final resting-place from all that wearies or troubles. It seems as though God in goodness had implanted this thought in all creatures' minds as the germ of eternal life, to cheer and support them in the shadowy hours of earth and time. Yes, the thought and hope of heaven is universal. Many men cherish ideas of hell, the very opposite of heaven; but this does not interfere with their own hope of heaven. All men hope for heaven for themselves. Hell is always for somebody else, if they are so unfortunate as to be tormented with so fearful and saddening a thought. And this thought of heaven, this universal impression of a better land, a spirit-bower, so comforting, so elevating, so inspiring, grows naturally out of our primary conceptions of Home. We all love Home—Home that is a Home—and this love enlarged by the imagination, pictured in perfection by the quick hand of Faith, consecrated by natural religion, is our idea of heaven. Heaven is Home perfected, the consummation of the heart's love of Home. In our ideas of heaven we gather our loved ones about us just as we do in our Homes. What would heaven be to us without our mother, our brothers and sisters, the dear home-companions of our hearts? It would not be heaven because it would not be Home. The heart could not rest there. It would fly away on the quick wings of its love to the dear absent ones. A heaven half filled would not be a heaven. A heaven with broken families would be heaven with broken hearts.

Every heart would pine in sadness in the loss of some of its dear ones—some of its Home souls. Home-love is the germ of heaven-love. God plants in Homes the seeds that shall bear fruit in heaven. Thus we see that *Mother*, *Home*, and *Heaven*—these three words of such universal interest and power—are associated and related words. They convey a blessed trinity of ideas meeting in one associated glow of spiritual beauty. They belong together and can not be separated. They are parts of the same golden whole. Home, in all well-constituted minds, is always associated with moral and social excellence. The higher men rise in the scale of being, the more important and interesting is Home. The Arab or forest man may care little for his Home, but the Christian man of cultured heart and developed mind will love his Home, and generally love it in proportion to his moral worth. He knows it is the planting-ground of every seed of morality—the garden of virtue, and the nursery of religion. He knows that souls immortal are here trained for the skies; that private worth and public character are made in its sacred retreat. To love Home with a deep and abiding interest, with a view to its elevating influence, is to love truth and right, heaven and God. I envy not the soul that loves not Home. There is moral safety and force in this love. Many a man who is an ornament to his family and a blessing to the world would have gone to ruin had it not been for the love he bore his Home and its inmates. A weakness of the home-love is often the cause of moral ruin. Many a man of strong impulses and impetuous character has braved hardships, faced dangers, resisted temptations which would have been too powerful for him had it not been for his strong love of Home. A strong love of Home in any man's heart is a triple wall of brass around his moral nature—an impregnable bulwark against the assaults of moral evil. No labor is too great for the strong lovers of Home to accomplish. See them on ocean's billowy bosom; on mountains of ice and snow; on fields of bloody strife; on burning deserts; in trackless forests; amid disease, danger, and death, braving every foe to life and peace, and all to fill their homes with comfort and joy. In every proper sense in which Home can be considered, it is a powerful stimulant to noble action and a high and pure morality. So valuable is the love of Home, that every man should cherish it as the apple of his eye. As he values his own moral worth, as he prizes his country, the peace and happiness of the world; yea, more: as he values the immortal interests of men, he should cherish and cultivate a strong and abiding love of Home.

I take it that it affects our whole lives; ay, that it runs over the grave, sweeps by death, and affects our future condition. Then is not the idea of Home important? Shall we look thoughtlessly upon these nurseries of immortal fruits? Shall we pollute and degrade the Homes in which we dwell? Shall we send out from them unholy influences to corrupt the world? These Home questions are the most important ones we can raise. Their decision is to affect us more than any decision by the supreme authority of our country. Not all the judges in the world ever decide questions half so important and pregnant with solemn results as those we are left to decide in our own Homes. Hence I would present the subject of Home to young women as one in which they are as deeply interested as they can be in any subject. It is expected that every young woman will preside over the destinies and interests of a Home. In some way her interests, through her whole earth-life, will be connected with Home. Woman's nature and tastes fit her in a peculiar manner to be the presiding genius of Home. However widely may be extended the rightful sphere of woman's operations, the mass of women will find employment and usefulness in the embosomment of their families.

Home will always, be woman's world. She will be queen over its rich and far-stretching realms. In the studios of Home she will carve the statuary of her moral heroism, and picture the spiritual beauty of her faith and love. Home is her kingdom, and she will always reign over it. Though she may go out to do great deeds of goodness in the world, though she may speak from forums, teach from college chairs, write books, fill offices of trust and profit, go on missions of truth, peace, and mercy among her fellows, she will still love best of all places the sequestered scene of Home. I would not, either by law, or custom, or public opinion, confine woman's powers to the routine of domestic duties. I would open the whole world to her, and tell her to find employment, usefulness, and happiness wherever she can; but in so doing I should feel that not a Home would be desolated; not a woman would become less a lover and blesser of Home. On the contrary, woman would love her Home all the more, and make it all the purer and nobler. She would choose its sweet vocations, not from the stern dictation of society, but from her soul's choice. Every family must have a Home; and every Home must have a head, a heart, a guardian. Woman is nobly fitted to fill this responsible post of honor and trust; but let her do it from choice. Do not compel her to do it. Woman does not like compulsion. It is not human to like compulsion. Give to woman the same freedom you do to man. Open the whole width of the field of life to her, and she will choose with avidity her own appropriate place. She has a strong sense of propriety and a good judgment in the choice of her sphere of activity.

Every young woman should early form in her mind an ideal of a *true Home.* It should not be the ideal of a *place,* but of the *character* of Home. Place does not constitute Home. Many a gilded palace and sea of luxury is not a Home. Many a flower-girt dwelling and splendid mansion lacks all the essentials of Home. A hovel is often more a Home than a palace. If the spirit of the congenial friendship link not the hearts of the inmates of a dwelling it is not a Home. If love reign not there; if charity spread not her downy mantle over all; if peace prevail not; if contentment be not a meek and merry dweller therein; if virtue rear not her beautiful children, and religion come not in her white robe of gentleness to lay her hand in benediction on every head, the Home is not complete. We are all in the habit of building for ourselves ideal homes. But they are generally made up of outward things—a house, a garden, a carriage, and the ornaments and appendages of luxury. And if in our lives we do not realize our ideals, we make ourselves miserable and our friends miserable. Half the women in our country are unhappy because their Homes are not so luxurious as they wish.

Somebody has more ornament and style about their Homes than they, and so they worry their souls to death about it. This is one of the most fruitful sources of disquiet in nearly all our Homes. Our women want more show, fashion, luxury, outward ornament than they can afford, or than is necessary to their happiness. All around us there is a great sea of disquiet from this one cause. We forget that Homes are not made up of material things. It is not a fine house, rich furniture, a luxurious table, a flowery garden, and a superb carriage that make a Home. A world-wide distance from this is a true Home. Our ideal Homes should be heart-Homes, in which virtues live, and love-flowers bloom, and peace offerings are daily brought to its altar. Our ideal Homes should be such as we can and will make in our own lives. We should not expect Homes better and happier than we are. Our Homes will be sure to be much like us. If we are good, kind, and happy, our Homes will be likely to be. If we are craving, selfish, discontented, our Homes will be. if all the wealth in the world were laid at our feet and lavished on our Homes, we should not be happier unless our hearts are better. Wealth, luxury, ornament bring care, anxiety, and a craving for more, which render them nearly valueless unless the heart is filled with virtue and contentment. If I could moderate the material desires of the young women I address, and elevate their spiritual longings in relation to their future Homes, I should do a good service to them and their families. The grand idea of Home is a quiet, secluded spot, where loving hearts dwell, set apart and dedicated to *improvement*—to intellectual and moral improvement. It is not a formal school of staid solemnity and rigid discipline, where virtue is made a task and progress a sharp necessity, but a free and easy exercise of all our spiritual limbs, in which obedience is a pleasure, discipline a joy, improvement a self-wrought delight. All the duties and labors of Home, when rightly understood, are so many means of improvement. Even the trials of Home (for every Home must have its trials, and severe ones, too) are so many rounds in the ladder of spiritual progress, if we but make them so.

One idea concerning Home should be deeply impressed on our minds. Of all places in the world, Home is the most delicate and sensitive. Its springs of action are subtile and secret. Its chords move with a breath. Its fires are kindled with a spark. Its flowers are bruised with the least rudeness. The influence of our homes strikes so directly on our hearts that they make sharp impressions. In our intercourse with the world we are barricaded, and the arrows let fly at our hearts are warded off; but not so with us at Home. Here our hearts wear no covering, no armor. Every arrow strikes them ; every cold wind blows full upon them ; every storm beats against them. What in the world we would pass by in sport, in our Homes will wound us to the quick. Very little can we bear at Home. Home is a sensitive place. If we would have it a true Home, we must guard well our words and actions. We must be honest and kind, constant and true, to the very extent of our capacity. All little occasions of offense and misapprehension should be avoided. Little things make up the web of our life at Home. Little things make us happy, and little things make us miserable. A word, a hint, a look has power to transport us with joy or sting us with anguish. If we would make our Homes what they should be, we must attend faithfully to the little things which make them so.

Our life abroad is but a reflex of what it is at Home. We make ourselves in a great manner at Home. This is especially true of woman. The woman who is rude, coarse, and vulgar at home, can not be expected to be amiable, chaste, and refined in the world. Her Home habits will stick to her. She can not shake them off. They are woven into the web of her life. Her Home language will be first on her tongue. Her Home by-words will come out to mortify her just when she wants most to hide them in her heart. Her Home vulgarities will show their hideous forms to shock her most when she wants to appear her best. Her Home coarseness will appear most when she is in the most refined circles, and appearing there will abash her more than elsewhere. All her Home habits will follow her. They have become a sort of second nature to her.

Every young woman should feel that just what she is at Home she will appear abroad. If she attempts to appear otherwise, everybody will soon see through the attempt. We can not cheat the world long about our real characters. The thickest and most opaque mask we can put on will soon become transparent. This fact we should believe without a doubt. Deception most often deceives itself. The deceiver is the most deceived. The liar is often the only one cheated. The young woman who pretends to what she is not, believes her pretense is not understood. Other people laugh in their sleeves at her foolish pretension.

If young women were what they ought to be at Home, they would never have to put on a mask when they go into company. How uncomfortable it must be to have to cover up the Home character the moment we appear in the world! Nothing should be said or done at Home that would make us appear in a bad light in the world. If this one rule is constantly kept, how pleasant will be our Homes, how proper our habits, how beautiful our lives! How easy and graceful will become our Home manners, how elegant and appropriate our Home language, how pure and lovely our Home characters! Home excellences are the ones we should covet. Home morality and religion are the best. Home love and worth only are real and lasting. Home virtue is for the skies. A Home woman of worth is the most beautiful and lovely woman in the world. A Home character is the one that will stand the scrutiny of the All-Seeing Eye. If these were the last words I had to say to young women, I would say, Be at Home what you would be abroad; what you ought to be everywhere; what all good people would have you; what God requires you to be.

Lecture Ten.

THE RELATIONS AND DUTIES OF YOUNG WOMEN TO YOUNG MEN.

The Primary Principles of Being—Life is full of Solemnities—Influence of the Sexes—Influence depends on Culture—Men Reverence Female Worth—Much Influence is directly Evil—Woman should demand Morality—Errors of Society—The Sexes too much Separated—Equality of Moral Standards—Female Encouragement and Counsel—Time Trifled, worse than Lost.

I FEEL that we have a subject before us of solemn and weighty importance. It relates to some of the dearest interests of our earth-life, gathers within itself some of the holiest affections of our hearts, and places before the bars of our consciences some of the most serious questions of practical morality and religion. Man and woman are a related pair. God has made them so. The relation they bear to each other is a divine one. It takes hold of the heart of life. It spans our whole manhood. It enters into our hopes, aims, and prospects. It holds its scepter over our business, our amusements, our philosophy, and religion. Its sphere is larger than we at first imagine. The relation is deeper and broader than we have yet comprehended. It lies in the very being of every man and every woman. There is in humanity two grand primary and universal principles of being—the masculine and feminine. They bear such a relation to each other that the one is essential to the action of the other. They mutually electrify and empower each other. It is in this mysterious relation that Infinite Wisdom has laid the springs of animate being. If any one mystery of our existence is deeper than any other, it is that which lies in the solemn depths of this relation. We ought to approach it wrapt in reverential awe and wonder. We look out on the earth in its brilliant beauty and teeming activity, and up to the heavens in their gorgeous glory and magnificent movements, and are oppressed with profound astonishment at what we behold. Yet all this we can in a measure comprehend. At least the secondary causes of the physical universe are clear to our minds. We can measure them with the line of mathematics; we can weigh them in the balance of reason. But when we turn in upon ourselves we meet a universe ten thousand times more wonderful and glorious, yet wrapt in the deep mystery of spiritual being. It is practical irreverence not to look upon our relations with religious respect. Of all these relations, the one between man and woman takes the most direct hold of our practical life and enters most largely into the details of our purposes and thoughts. Men and women live in and for each other more than for any thing else. The fact stands out on the face of human society. We must take the fact as we find it. We did not make human nature; hence we have no right to complain of it. Our business is to comprehend it so far as possible and seek to keep it in the path of its design and destiny. Our morality and religion should be adapted to our nature. They should meet the every-day wants of men.

The philosopher, the moralist, and the minister should aim at practical utility in all their labors, and men and women should study carefully the great book of every-day life. The relation of men and women to each other is one of the most important lessons in that book. If we would be wise, useful, or happy, we must understand at least the *duties* growing out of this relation. If we would bless mankind or please God, we must fulfill these duties. I have but little faith in any philosophy or religion that would shun the walks of practical life. We have too much ethereal philosophy and spasmodic religion. Men reason profoundly about etherealities, and go into ecstasies about glory and joy to come. This may be all well enough, but I submit whether it would not be better to reason how to live well the life that now is, and how to sanctify it with the redeeming presence of the spirit of the lowly Jesus. Our chief concern is with this life. If we make it right, no harm can come to us in the future life. To me our present life is full of holy solemnities. Its most interesting relations are holy, and the duties that grow out of them are to be performed with religious sincerity and joy. To me God is in our present life, walking with us daily and entreating us to walk with him. I see His arrangement in the relation of man and woman. I feel his benediction in the joy and blessed influence that arise from this relation. I can not consider it or enjoy it in any other than a religious sense. Nor can I conceive of any true religion in the heart of him who practically sinks this relation to a level with sensualism or folly. I hear almost daily from the lips of professedly religious men and women, language and thoughts on this subject which bespeak a carnal heart and an unsanctified mind. They treat the relation with levity. They make it a practical joke. They look at it through carnal eyes, and listen to its language with carnal ears. Their whole conception and practical understanding of it is sensuous. I have but little confidence in their religion. It is only an emotion of the heart. It has never sanctified the conscience nor consecrated the life.

With these introductory remarks let us observe in the first place, that the most potent influence that bears on our earth-life grows out of this relation. This is a fact standing out boldly on the face of life. And this influence is more powerful in refined and cultured life than in savage and primitive existence. As individuals, nations, and races advance in the arts, principles, and culture of civilization, the influence of the sexes becomes more general and irresistible. So far as a people advance morally, religiously, and spiritually, this influence becomes more direct, constant, and powerful. The truest men and the truest women we have are most under each other's influence. They bow most reverently in each other's presence and entertain the highest opinions of each other. Their feelings toward each other are most pure and truthful. One of the most intellectual, religious, and refined women that it has been my privilege to meet in life's sequestered vale, while speaking in a private conversation, made this significant remark: Next to my God do I adore man, for he is God's best image." She was a matronly woman about sixty years of age, who had tasted life's full cup and been blessed by its richest and most profound experiences, and who said of her religion: "For twenty-five years it has been my meat and my drink." It is a joy and a blessing never to be forgotten to have known such a woman. The best men I have ever known, considered both in relation to their spiritual experiences and their influence in life, have joyfully and reverently expressed their feelings of profound respect and sacred affection for woman, confessing that, under God, she had wrought in them a mission of redeeming love. So frequent have been similar expressions both from men and women in the highest spiritual and practical walks in life, and so clear and strong has been their experience, that it can not be doubted that the influence of man and woman upon each other is potent and penetrating in proportion to their degree of refinement and spiritual culture. The tendency of moral training and religious discipline are to strengthen and elevate this influence.

Woman improves in man's view as her nature is cultivated and her soul blessed with sanctifying influences. Man grows in woman's sight as his mind is developed and his heart subdued. They mutually exert a higher and deeper influence over each other by their progress in things good and true. If I am correct in this, it presents us with a strong inducement to develop our best powers and live our best lives, that our mental joys may be most deep and holy and our lives most pure and happy. And here I may present the subject directly to young women. If they would secure the deepest respect and holiest friendship of the young men with whom they associate, they must themselves be refined, elevated, and noble in their characters and lives. If they would exert their best influence upon young men, and benefit them most by their association with them, they must be truthful and high of soul.

All young men bow before female worth. Their evil thoughts forsake them; their wicked habits flee away from them for the time being. Let a depraved man *feel* that he stands in the presence of pure, cultivated womanhood, around which is wrapped the mantle of Jesus, and through which breathes the spirit of his holy religion, and he will be ashamed of himself, and long to be sufficiently pure and elevated to commune in sacred friendship with her spirit. Oh, if young women could only realize the moral powers which they could gather up within themselves, and wield over their male associates in all the walks of life, by a proper development of their minds and hearts, and a truthful submission to the principles of moral right, how different would they be, and how changed would be the face of young society! That young women do wield a mighty influence over young men we admit; but it is not so great nor so good as it should be. Much of it is directly evil. It is trifling, deceitful, volatile, changeable, and not unfrequently carnal. It is often low, worldly, irreverent, base. I am sorry to say it, but young women rebuke but very little the evil doings of their male associates. They chide not the waywardness of young men as they ought. They smile upon them in their villainy. They court the society of young men they have every reason to believe are corrupt. They will meet without a shudder or disapproving frown, in the ball-room and the private circle, men whom they know would glory in being the instrument of the moral ruin of any woman. Young women who claim to be good, and who would not for a fortune be guilty of a moral impropriety, often wreathe the villain's way in smiles.

Young men in "high life" can smoke and chew, drink and swear, in woman's presence, and she turns not away in disgust nor rebukes them with a cut of their acquaintance. There are a large class of young women who only ask that the young men shall behave tolerably well in their presence, asking not what they do behind their backs. They may carouse, blaspheme, get drunk, and do what wickedness they please among themselves; if they only keep straight in the ladies' presence, it is all that is asked. Now there is by far too much of this low state of morality among young women. I say among young women, because if their moral feelings were what they should be, they would not associate with such young men. They would not enroll them on their list of friends. They would not know their names; would not recognize them when they met. I have no confidence in the moral sense of young women who will acknowledge such associates. The very first duty which women owe to young men is to demand of them a higher standard of morality. I say *demand*. They should peremptorily demand it. Young women should erect the standard for young men which young men have erected for them. Young men who have any respect for themselves will not associate with women that chew, and smoke, and swear, and get drunk—those whose morals are low and base. They spurn such associates from them. Let young women do the same. Let them say to the young men, "You shall not do the things you prohibit us from doing; you shall not, behind our backs, do things you would despise us for doing; you shall not bring into our society characters from which you know every honest and pure woman ought to recoil as she would from a basilisk; you shall not breathe into our faces the pestiferous breath of the drunkard, nor burden our ears with the hateful sound of the blasphemer; you must be what you would have us, or you must be out of our society." Let young women talk thus and act thus, and true young men will respect them all the more. No woman is respected more for smiling on the villain. He himself despises her for it. The truth is, our society is corrupt on this subject. *Men* are permitted to do with impunity what would blast a woman's reputation for life. A man may be coarse, vulgar, and wicked, and society admits him to all its privileges, and good women will meet him on terms of equality. Society can never be what it should be till the same standard of morality and propriety is established for men and women. It is woman's duty to establish such a standard—a duty she owes to man. She does man an act of injustice when she accepts him as an associate at the sacrifice of her moral dignity. It is her duty to rebuke his evil course. It is kindness to him to do it.

Young women can not do a bad man a greater evil than to associate with him on terms of moral equality. All young women should show by their words and actions that they have a deep and holy respect for moral worth; that they will demand it in their associates. Such a course would inspire a greater respect for them in the minds of young men, and give a higher tone to the moral feelings of our youth.

It is a well-settled conviction of my mind that society separates too much its male and female youth. In our schools our boys and girls are separated. Almost the entire course of education is pursued in sexual isolation. The girls are taught that it is not pretty to be with the boys, and the boys that is not manly to be with the girls; and yet both are anxious for each other's society. In this unnatural and unhappy state, their imaginations are left to fill up the void made by the separation. Imagination seldom does such work well. I believe it is the grand corrupter of youth. The brother and sister should grow up together in the same family, be educated at the same school, engage in the same sports, and, so far as practical, in the same labors. Their joys and sorrows, tastes and aims, should be mutual so far as possible. The same moral lessons, the same moral obligations and duties should bear upon them. The moral standard for the girl should be the moral standard for the boy, and he should be made to feel that the moment he falls below it he is unworthy, and must not expect her confidence and society. It is a sad error that the youth of our towns and country are separated in so many of the most important duties of life. They are permitted to come together only for sport and nonsense. Their study and work are separate. Hence the good influence which they ought to have upon each other is in a great measure lost. They are unacquainted with each other. They know not each other's natures. They have but little interest in each other's business and duties. They meet only to cajole and deceive each other. They wear masks in each other's presence. For this state of things no one in particular is to blame, but every one in general. It is the fault of society. Now it seems to me to be a duty of every young woman to seek to correct this state of things, by acquainting herself as far as possible with the interests and business of young men that she may seek to benefit them by her approval of what is right and condemnation of what is wrong.

If woman was more intimately acquainted with the life, duty, hopes, and aims of man, with his business, his education, his sharp encounters, his trials and temptations, she could be of much more service to him intellectually, morally, and socially. I do not believe in the present isolation of woman from man's business, ambition, and hope. Woman might be a perpetual inspiration to man to act nobly his part in the theater of life if she knew that part and was more deeply interested in it. And here is just where young women can be of great service to young men. In nearly all young men there is more or less of noble ambition, of praiseworthy aim for an active and useful life. Some wish to fill posts of honor and trust in their country's service ; some would win respect and honor in some of the learned professions ; some would seek esteem and competency in the schools of art ; some would lay the foundations of a noble life in mechanism ; some in agriculture ; some in commerce. The avocations are many, but the spirit, the aim, the ambition is one. In these avocations young men expect to make their fortunes, win their fame, work out their good, and do their life-work. If young women had their hearts in these things, saw the true end of life, and would enter into the young man's plans and hopes, they might cheer and animate, encourage and empower, thousands of young men who otherwise will make grand failures of life. How little encouragement, how little counsel and cheer do young men now get from their young female associates ! What young woman enters heartily into the best aims and highest hopes of the young man with whom she associates ?

What young woman watches with anxious and benevolent solicitude the young men about her, in relation to their success and progress in the vocations and pursuits to which their lives are wedded, and from which their fortunes, characters, and spiritual good are in no small degree to be made ? Our young women are too childish and trifling in their thoughts and intercourse with young men. They seek to dissipate rather than benefit them; or, if they do not seek it, their intercourse tends to dissipation. It should not be so. All of woman's influence should tend to elevate man. He is bad enough, do all she can for him. The hours she spends with him should be for his inspiration; to make him more active in the pursuit of whatever is noble in life or good in spirit.

Every hour trifled away with young men is an hour worse than lost. It injures both parties. Woman exerts a great influence over man. She should see to it that that influence is good. She should encourage him in all his intellectual pursuits, throw the whole weight of her influence upon his moral nature, resolutely demand a good life at his hands, and electrify his laudable purposes with the strength of her holiest prayer. She may be to him an angel of redeeming mercy. She may magnetize his soul with strength. She may gird him with the armor of religion and make him a soldier of the Cross, braver than Cæsar and mightier than Napoleon. But to do it she must herself be strong in the right. She must be panoplied in the armor of spiritual warfare. She must be a true woman, girded and crowned with the royalty of noble womanhood. Being this, she must ask her brother to wear the royal badge of high-toned manhood. Let young women learn how men are made; how, by industry, labor, prudence, perseverance in the common vocations of life, and by a strict adherence to rectitude and goodness they grow to be useful and great, and then they may become ministers of good to the rising manhood of our country.

I have great hopes in young woman. The destinies of the generations to come are not a little in her hands. In the stirring times that are before us she must act a noble part. Her pen, her voice, her power will move upon the world. Every young woman will do something in this movement. Let her determine to do her part well; to be a true woman; to lead a true life; to exert a true influence on mankind in the fear of God and the love of man.

Lecture Eleven.

MARRIAGE.

Unhappy Marriages—Marriage has its Laws—The Second Question in Life—Be sure you are Right—For Better or for Worse—Know whom thou Marriest—Marriage a Holy Institution—Marriage should be made a Study—Marriage is not for Children—Early Marriages Unadvisable—What are Early Marriages?—Influence of an Ignorant Wife—Woman the Hope of the World—Married Life must be lived well—Love should rule all.

OUR present theme for our young female friends is Marriage. In treating it we feel impressed with its solemn and practical importance. Talk of Marriage as we will, it is a serious and stern reality. It takes us by the hand and leads us into the great temple of life where duties stand ministering around the solemn altar, and the baptism of love is followed by the quick discipline of trial. Young, single existence is but the vestibule of real life, where anticipation weaves a golden web, bearing but a faint resemblance to the web of actual life. The youthful imagination is apt to dress the institution of Marriage in too many garlands, and to consider it full of ethereal joys and paradisiacal blessedness such as can exist only in the chambers of an untaught fancy. That the natural fruitage of true Marriage is peace and blessedness is a pleasing fact which we can not contemplate but with delight, and for which we can not be too grateful. But it must always be understood that the joys of marriage are natural, and such as grow out of the performance of duty and a life of truthfulness. They are conditioned upon obedience to the matrimonial laws. It is not all the married that are happy. If you would find misery double-distilled, you may find it in awful and ruinous abundance among the married who entered their real life in the whirl of enthusiastic delight. There is every possible degree of anguish in the married life, from the unbreathed unrest of the thinly clouded soul to the terrible grief that breaks out in loud denunciations and open and disgusting conflict. And could you draw back the vail that hides the privacies of this life, and see the black waves of distrust and the deep waters of disquietude that cast up mire and dirt continually, which roll and heave in constant commotion out of the world's sight in the seclusion of the Marriage relation, you might doubt that the institution was ordained in mercy, and question its utility. Like every other good, it must be rightly used or it turns to evil. The good of good things is mostly in their use. Life is good if rightly used, but oh, how bad when wholly abused! So with Marriage. The best things become instruments of the direst evil when wrested from their true use.

The first lesson to learn in relation to Marriage is, that its fruits of peace and joy hang on the boughs of obedience to its regulations, conformity to its laws. Who would be happy in the married life must enter into it well and live it righteously. It has laws to be obeyed, regulations to be observed, principles to be submitted to, without which it has no joys, no elysian fields of bliss and blessedness, no buds and flowers of virtue and happiness.

It will never do to go blindly into a state of such intimate relations. Here soul meets with soul face to face. Propensities, passions, desires, inclinations, aspirations, capacities, powers, stand up side by side and press against each other, either to please or fret and chafe each other. Tastes, dispositions, feelings, either join in sweet, according friendship, or rankle in disagreeable contact. Marriage is a union, intimate, strong-bound, and vitally active. The union is a compound or a mixture; it is natural, congenial, pleasing, or it is forced, inharmonious, and revolting. Which it shall be we are to determine before we enter it. We are not to shut our eyes to reason and common sense, and marry whoever offers. Young women who do so may live to repent it. If there is any period in a woman's whole life when her sharpest eye, her keenest apprehension, her soundest judgment, and her most religious seriousness are needed, it is when she proposes to herself the question, "Shall I accept in marriage the hand that is offered me?" It is the second greatest question of her life. It is the question, the answer of which is to wring briny tears out of her heart or baptize it in the waters of refreshing sympathy.

I once knew a merchant who used to say that "Goods well bought were half sold." The idea is equally good when applied to the subject of Marriage. A Marriage well entered is a life half lived. It is hard to make a profit on badly bought goods. So it is hard to live a good and happy life in Marriage bonds that bind and gall the heart that wears them. I used to be a farmer, and I then learned that a balky horse would often work well in an easy harness, while a good horse would be tricky and stubborn in a collar that chafed. So I have often seen bad people who lived very happily in the married life, so far as their personal relations were concerned, while good people chafed and grieved in sad matrimonial inharmony. Half the victory is in starting the battle right. A man of more good sense than refinement once said, "Be sure you are right, then go ahead." It is the utterance of wisdom, and is as applicable to the subject before us as any other. "Be sure you are right." We are not only to be right, but we are to know it. There is to be no guess-work about it —no wish-work or hope-work about it. It is to be knowledge-work. Applied to the subject in hand, young women are to know that they are right in their Marriage alliances; are to know that they have bargained with men after their own heart. They are not to guess they are going to get pretty good husbands, nor hope they are, nor to believe they are from what personal friends have said.

They are not to rely upon common report, nor the opinion of friends, nor a fashionable acquaintance, but upon a personal knowledge of the individual's life and character. How can another know what you want in a companion? You alone know your own heart. If you do not know it you are not fit to be married. No one else can tell what fills you with pleasing and grateful emotions. You only know when the spring of true affection is touched by the hand of a congenial spirit. It is for you to *know* who asks your hand, who has your heart, who links his life with yours. If you *know* the man who can make true answer to your soul's true love, whose soul is all kindred with yours, whose life answers to your ideal of manly demeanor, you know who would make you a good husband. But if you only fancy that he is right, or guess, or believe, or hope, from a little social interchange of words and looks, you have but a poor foundation on which to build hopes of future happiness. A young man and a dear friend once said to me, "I am going to take her for better or for worse." The remark ran over me like a chill breath of winter. I shuddered at the thought. "For better or for worse." All in doubt. Going to marry, yet not *sure* he was right. The lady he spoke of was a noble young woman, intellectual, cultivated, pious, accustomed to his sphere of life. They were going to marry in uncertainty. Both were of fine families; both excellent young people. To the world it looked like a desirable match. To them it was going to be "for better or for worse." They married. The woman stayed in his home one year and left it, declaring he was a good man and a faultless husband, but not after her heart. She stayed away one year and came back; lived with him one year more and died. Sad tale. It proved for the worse, and all because they did not *know* each other; if they had they would not have married. I once heard of a woman who married a man to get rid of him. It is a dangerous riddance. Equally dangerous is it to marry a man to find him out. "*Know* whom thou *marriest*," is the voice of wisdom. Yes, the question of Marriage is one of solemn import. It is a life-question. It is a final settlement of a great demand of our nature. It is the decision of the heart's earthly weal or woe. It is our social life or death. It is planting the seeds for the moral harvest of life. It is the adjustment of a great religious question, the submission to a solemn ordinance of God. Yes, Marriage is a divine institution. It is not of earthly origin, though it is often prostituted to earthly uses. It is a God-made arrangement for human development and happiness, and wo be to him who defiles it with sensuous abuses. It is before the Church, before any of the solemn ordinances of God's house, the primal decree of the Father for his human children. To degrade or abuse the Marriage covenant is blasphemy, irreverence, sacrilegious wickedness. If one would enter the portals of the church bowed in reverence to God, much more should he thus enter the sanctuary of Marriage. If he should sit reverently at the table of the Lord's Supper, much more should he sit thus in the bower of the hymeneal life. If he should bow his head in solemn meekness in the baptismal rite, much more should he bend lowly in this relation. If he should kneel in pious prayer before the throne of grace, so he should humble himself before God at the life-union altar. There is no more serious step in life, none more important, and none that should be more religiously taken.

In this view of the subject, what a sad picture does the

world present! How trifling, giddy, thoughtless! Among the multitudes who marry, how few marry in the light of wisdom and under the sanction of religion! Worldliness moves a great multitude in the formation of this union. Profit, gain, standing! These are mighty things. Principle, virtue, religion, happiness, must be sacrificed on the altar of worldly ambition. Woman becomes a base creature by thus pandering to earthly ends. Then worse than this, still greater multitudes are prompted to this union by sensuous desires—base animalism. Oh, to what a sink of iniquity, what a pool of pollution, what a stagnant pit of moral rottenness is the Marriage relation sunk by the unhallowed and unbridled sensuality of thousands who enter it! If there is any place in the world where the voice of God should be heard ringing in pealing thunder-tones the commands of virtue and religion, it is in the seclusion of the Marriage relation. Men, and women, too, ought to look to Marriage with a profounder respect and a higher purpose. It is a holy institution. To degrade it is wicked and brings the most bitter unhappiness. If I should induce a single young woman to look more reverently upon the life-union, to regard it in its moral and religious aspects, and determine to enter it under the sanctions of true religion, and demand a like state of mind in her companion, that they might live to be blessings to each other, I should feel richly remunerated for my labor. I treat this subject now and have at former times with a view to elevate the minds of youth in relation to it.

It is in vain to try to make the world moral and religious

while the great institutions of social life are corrupted and corrupting. At the very bottom of adult life lies the institution of Marriage. To reform the world we must begin with this. If we can get men and women well married, the work of reform is half done; life is half lived. It is next to impossible to make good and happy an ill-assorted pair. They work against each other almost in spite of themselves. They are like a steamboat with its wheels playing in opposite directions. They make a great noise and a terrible jarring, and put forth desperate efforts, but no forward motion is produced.

It would be well if we had more judicious books on Marriage, designed for youth. One on the Philosophy of Marriage; one on the Duties of Marriage; one on the Religion of Marriage; or all these subjects treated in one book might be very profitable; and if such a book were designed for high schools, academies, and colleges, and made a study, as is moral science and natural religion, it might be made eminently useful. There is a science of Marriage. It should be developed and made a study. Some strong mind and pure heart, baptized in the spirit of divine truth and love, should write it out. I know the youth of our country would receive it gladly and study it with great profit. What is most wanted is thought and enlightenment on the subject. Thought is the grand lever of reform. This thing of thinking is what makes men great and good. It is the grand plowshare that turns up the old soil of error and despotism and reveals the hidden treasures of truth. Get people to thinking and they will be likely to think themselves right in the end. We want thought on the subject of Marriage—calm, consecutive, serious thought. Nothing else will do. We have passion, zeal, impulse, imagination; but we lack thought. Thought is the helm of passion, the ballast of imagination, the compass of impulse. Let youth think on the subject as they ought, and they will marry well.

I remarked that the institution of Marriage was at the bottom of adult life. This is a truth, and it is a thought for the girls. Marriage was never designed for children. It is for men and women. It is good for men and women; but it does not follow from this that it is good for children. It would not be good even if children knew how to marry wisely. They are both physically and mentally incapacitated for so solemn and important a relation. They are immature in body and mind, in heart and head. Their judgments are unsound. Their affections are not to be trusted. They are children in every sense of the word, and can only make children's work of married life. The wisest and best in early adult life can be none too well prepared for the great duties of married life—how can children be prepared? It is impossible. One of the greatest evils of our time is the too prevalent custom of entering early into the Marriage relations. Children make bad selections of companions. In nine cases out of ten they choose differently from what they would a few years later. They have no fixed characters. They do not know what their opinions will be. Their tastes are not formed. Their aims in life are undetermined. What they were made for and what they live for they have scarcely asked. The arguments against early Marriages are many. I have not time to enumerate them or to show their force. I have never heard of but one argument in favor of early marriages. That is founded in the false idea of marrying in mutual ignorance of each other. It is said the characters of the parties are more pliable in early youth, so that they will assimilate to each other the more readily. But if they are not already assimilated they ought not to marry. If each has got to give up his character to live in peace, it is a proof that they are wrongly matched. Those really fitted for each other find their happiness in the harmony of each other's characters. Their two characters blend together like concordant sounds, or two streams of running water. The secret of true Marriage is in mutuality of character, harmony of sentiment and action, congeniality of spirit. Without this unity there can be no true Marriage; no real happiness or utility in the married life.

In all true Marriages the twain become one; one in feeling, aim, and spirit, one in reason, sentiment, and love. And when this does not exist before Marriage, it can not reasonably be looked for after. That this harmony shall be perfect we can not expect, because there are no perfect characters in this world, and no two persons at perfect unity in spirit. But unless there is a general harmony there should be no Marriage. Now, how can children know whether this harmony exists, when their own characters are unformed, their powers undeveloped? But it may be asked, what we call an early Marriage? About this there may be a difference of opinion. What some would call early, others would call late. Our ideas on this point should be founded in physiological and mental science. There is a true test by which to settle this question. That test is found in the human constitution. Any Marriage is early that is consummated before adult womanhood is attained—womanhood of mind, heart, soul, and character. Any Marriage before eighteen years of age is a very early Marriage; before twenty it is early. As a general rule, between twenty and twenty-five it is timely, though with many it is early at twenty-two, and some never get old enough to marry. A mind untaught, a heart undisciplined, a spirit unsubdued, in a civilized community, is not fit to be married. Such a character is never old enough.

Above all things, before Marriage, there should be time enough for a generous education; for a wise preparation for practical life. No young woman can be educated in any practical and general sense before twenty-two, no matter what may be her opportunities. Life ought to be understood; its practical aspects should be fairly and wisely contemplated; its principal duties should be well weighed; its trials, temptations, and besetments should be considered; all that must be done and borne should be the subject of thoughtful meditation before a woman should dare to set her foot upon the hallowed ground of matrimony. No child is capable of considering such grave subjects. An adult mind is scarcely equal to the task.

When I say young women should have time to be educated, I mean all young women. It is true, all will not be educated in our schools, but all must have some sort of an education; they must have some experience, observation, contact with men and things, a knowledge of life; must learn to rely upon themselves, and learn moral duty and what the world expects of a wife. The early married must also necessarily be married in ignorance; and as a general rule we may say, who marries in ignorance will remain in ignorance. An ignorant wife! Poor thing! How sad the spectacle! What can she do with life? She will make an ignorant mother and rear ignorant children, and exert an ignorant influence all through her life. She will perpetuate the absurdities of ignorant people. She will do the work of ignorance with her husband and family. Still worse is a neighborhood of ignorant wives. A State of ignorant wives would bring barbarism again. And how could it be otherwise, if all girls should marry in their girlhood? It is the girls that live to womanhood before they marry that redeem and polish society. Those who marry in girlhood are drawbacks on society. They are dead weights holding back the wheels of progress. There are but few truly educated and influential women in the country who married before they were twenty-five—many of them not till after. They are now the pride and glory of their husbands, of the communities and States in which they live. I hold that a noble and influential woman is an honor to the country and a pillar of civil and religious liberty. Every such woman is a central sun radiating intellectual and moral light, diffusing strength and life to all about her. The hope of the country—ay, of the world—is in its women; I may say its wives. Now and then a wife will develop and educate herself after she is married, if she is fortunate enough to get a husband who will encourage and help her in the work, even if she is married young; but the great mass will remain in *statu quo*. If they marry ignorant they will remain ignorant. I can not press too strongly this point of preparation for Marriage.

There is more depends upon it than we at first imagine. Every wife is to be the center of a family. Boys and girls, men and women, are to go out from her to live in the world. Scan it closely and you will find that the world will be modeled very much after its wives. If we have great and good men, great and good institutions, States and countries, it is because we have great and good wives. A wife will be happy just about in proportion to the amount of good she does. That amount of good will depend very much upon the education of her girlhood; so that view it in whatever light we will, a woman's life, usefulness, and happiness depend in no small degree upon the length and character of her girlhood. If she remains unmarried till she is twenty-three or twenty-five, and develops and cultivates herself as she ought, she will be almost sure to make a good and useful woman, an ornament and an inspiration to the circle in which she moves. If she marries at sixteen or eighteen she will be very likely to make just what she is—an immature, unfinished specimen of humanity; nothing more, nothing less.

One point more I would dwell upon a moment. It is this: The married life, though entered never so well, and with all proper preparation, must be lived well or it will not be useful or happy. Married life will not go itself, or if it does it will not keep the track. It will turn off at every switch, and fly off at every turn or impediment. It needs a couple of good conductors who understand the engineering of life. Good watch must be kept for breakers ahead. The fires must be kept up by a constant addition of the fuel of affection. The boilers must be kept full and the machinery in order, and all hands at their posts, else there will be a smashing up, or life will go hobbling or jolting along, wearing and tearing, breaking and bruising, leaving some heads and hearts to get well the best way they can. It requires skill, prudence, and judgment to lead this life well, and these must be tempered with forbearaace, charity, and integrity. Individual rights, opinions, and feelings must be respected; individual duties must be faithfully performed; the proprieties of courtesy and kindness must be most strictly observed; violations of politeness and affection must be prohibited; ebullitions of temper must be considered as sad and lamentable improprieties, to be mourned over but always quickly and readily forgiven; the motto of each should be, "I will *be*, *do*, and *bear* all I can and ask as little as possible." A constant and perfect agreement in opinion and feeling between the parties must never be expected. The rule should be, that they will agree just so far as possible without a violation of the individual conscience, and when they can not agree further they should agree to disagree, with mutual respect for each other's opinions and mutual esteem and love for each other. Neither one should attempt or wish to set up a petty and matrimonial tyranny over the other. Each should think, feel, and act in kindly independence; and each should encourage the other in independent thought and action with a view to individual culture and mutual benefit. But below all thought and back of all action there should be a strong, earnest, two-fold principle of benevolence and affection. Come what may, love should rule over all. This should pervade and magnetize the whole life. Love should utter its melodious tones and breathe its sweet spirit in every department of the united life. This is the life that should be determined upon before Marriage this the life that the parties should mark out for themselves in all its detail, before they enter into the Marriage covenant; and this the life when lived that is blessed and blissful beyond expression.

I said in the outset of this discourse that the young are apt to hang too many garlands about the married life. This is so as this life is generally lived. But if it is wisely entered and truthfully lived, it is more beautiful and happy than any have imagined. It is the true life which God has designed for his children, replete with joy, delightful, improving, and satisfactory in the highest possible earthly degree. It is the hallowed home of virtue, peace, and bliss. It is the antechamber of heaven, the visiting place of angels, the communing ground of kindred spirits. Let all young women who would reap such joys and be thus blessed and happy, learn to live the true life, and be prepared to weave for their brows the true wife's perennial crown of goodness

Lecture Twelve.

RELIGIOUS DUTIES.

Our Father in Heaven—Moral Obligations and Religious Duties—Impiety of Professed Christians—Deficiency of Religious Gratitude—Gratitude makes Life Cheerful—Religion gives Joy to Life—Love, the Seed of Religion—The Religion of Christ—Woman's Heart a Natural Shrine—Religion fit for all Conditions—Love for the Unseen—Personal Acquaintance not necessary for Love—The Idea of God Spontaneous—It is the Unseen we Love—Life well lived is Glorious.

We propose a few thoughts in the present Lecture to young women upon their *Religious Duties*. The theme is a rich one. Any consideration of our relations and duties to the great Father of all, the Lord Almighty, the primal source of being and blessing, is replete with moral grandeur. God is a great and glorious word, expressive of all infinities, all perfections, all glories, word of all words, in power and grandeur above all. It should inspire us with reverence. The thought of that incomprehensible Being, which we mean by this word, should ever impress us with moral solemnity. And when we associate with this majestic Being the idea of Father, clothe him in a Father's love, fill him with a Father's care and benignity, he appears to us infinitely lovely and attractive as well as infinitely great and good. It is no common thought that gives to the universe of spiritual creatures a Father, that binds them all in one family with God as the head, that mingles in the great cup of universal existence of which countless millions of sentient beings are daily partaking, the sweetness of a father's goodness ; that sees that goodness in the shining sun and falling shower, in the starry firmament and the little flower, in the sweep of worlds and the drop of dew, in the waving grain and the bubbling spring, in the changing seasons and the still, calm moments as they fly, in the great race of men, and in the individual members thereof. We often say "Our Father in Heaven," but we seldom think of the majesty of the expression, nor the glorious beauty of the thought it conveys. God's grandeur is as much in his love as his power, as much in his goodness as his wisdom. He is as sublime in his Fatherhood as in his supremacy. The ocean of his tenderness is as deep as the mountain of his holiness is high. God, in his character, sweeps over the infinite spaces of principle and gathers in the infinite perfections of all characteristics of good. It is to such a Being that we owe our existence and all that makes it blessed and blissful. When we think of the earth as our present home, so wisely arranged, so beautifully adorned, and of heaven as our final and immortal scene of growing joy and blessedness ; when we think of our own wonderful powers of mind and heart, and the objects of love and thought about us upon which to exercise them, progressive, immortal, Godlike in their nature ; when, added to these, we think of the Bible with its blessed and elevating relations, its love of truth, its mines of wisdom, its moral sanctions, and, more than all, its Divine Redeemer, our Pattern Friend, Brother, and Saviour, we can not well fail to be impressed with the infinite excellency of Him from whom we have received such rich benefactions.

And when we think that all this is done for us of his own unpurchased love, our obligations to our Divine Father become clear to our moral perceptions. We then see that we have religious duties to perform, duties which press upon us at all seasons and places, duties which we must perform, or stand before the great white throne of Eternal Love convicted of deep and dark ingratitude. We have received every thing, and have the promise of every thing, and have given nothing. We have been loved with an infinite affection, and have the promise of its everlasting continuance, and yet many of us have not returned the poor affections of our feeble finite hearts. We have been over-arched with the firmament of immortal goodness all our lives long, and have the promise that it shall span us forever, and yet we have drank in but little of its life and light. We have fed on the bounties of a benignant Providence and have scarcely returned an emotion of genuine thoughtfulness. Here we are; God is all the time doing for us; and we are thoughtless of his favors and indifferent to his holy friendship. He strives to impress us with his greatness, but we scarcely seem to recognize the entreaties of his love or the munificence of his bountiful hand Through His love he pleads in the earnest eloquence of a divine life and a perfect heart for us to bow in love at the feet of Jesus; but even those of us who profess to do so are cold in our love and weak in our resolutions. The world has stolen away our hearts. Evil associates have corrupted our good manners, and we are irreverent, sensuous, even in the house of God. To illustrate our impiety: suppose you, by some accident, had been cast away on some lone island, barrenness reigned around you; cold winds beat against you; alone and desolate you stood exposed to every element without and a prey to every want within. The sea in its wild fury roared around you. No living being heard your cries; no heart beat in sympathy with yours. Now, suppose in your distress a good spirit of the island should speak to you, out of a cell or cloud, and ask your wants; and should lead you into a beautiful temple, and tell you it was yours; should feed and clothe you; should surround you with beauty and comfort, furnish you with friends, and make every thing delightful so far as another could do for you, what kind of feelings ought you to entertain toward the good spirit? If you should forget him in your enjoyments, should abuse his gifts, should make him the subject of jest and sport, and blaspheme his name, would you not, in your thoughtful moments, despise yourself for your ingratitude? And yet this good spirit, in the supposed case, would not do for you a tithe your heavenly Father is doing for you every day; for life, and breath, and powers, all natural as well as spiritual things, we receive at his hand.

Few things are more base than an ungrateful spirit.

If we do a favor either to a friend or stranger, and get no response of gratitude, we feel that something is wrong in his heart. Ingratitude we name among the most hateful feelings that ever darken the fallen heart of humanity. It is the parent of innumerable vices. It is a cold, Satanic mood of mind, suggestive of numberless forms of evil. And yet, unless I greatly mistake, there is much ingratitude in all our hearts. We eat, and forget the Hand that feeds us. We wear, and heed not the Adorner of our persons. We admire our bodies, and offer not an emotion of praise to the grand Architect of the universe and its beauty. We rejoice in our strength and comeliness, scarcely thinking that we owe it all to the Divine love. We delight in our domestic relations and affections, and often grow eloquent in praise of the sweet emotions of delicious joy which rise within us, half forgetting that they are all gifts from the gracious Divinity.

We grow proud in the might of our minds, and vain of our works, bloating often to the bursting point, claiming all the glory to ourselves, awarding little or none to God. This is lamentably true to an alarming extent. It is true of youth as well as manhood. Though youth is brimful of good impulses and quick affections, it is sadly deficient in religious gratitude. It is right that young people should enjoy the good things of life and the world, should make merry with each other, and even be gay amid the profusion of natural gayety about them, but in doing so they need not and should not be unmindful of their good Father in heaven. First in their affections, highest in their joyful adoration should He stand. God is a parent. In this light should He be regarded. To be grateful to a parent for favors received does not interfere with the natural buoyancy of the heart. To love a parent does not make less active and cheerful the love we bear others, nor gloom our lives with one single cloud. The young woman who loves her father with an earnest affection, will not love any body else less, but more. The young man who loves his mother with his whole soul, who at all times and places, amid all pleasures and amusements, retains her image in his heart of hearts, and turns to her ever as the refreshing fountain of his sweetest joy, is none the less capable of loving all his fellow-men. On the contrary, the love he bears his mother will be the seed from which will grow a grand tree of love, the branches and freshness of which will fill his whole heart and beautify his whole life. If a young man loves his mother truly, he is safe for a good life. In the end his love will conquer all and bear off the crown of victory. So of a young woman. This love of parents is among the healthiest and noblest feelings of the heart. It seems to be the germinating point of both affection and virtue. It is both a guard against evil and an inspiration to good. It is more than simple love, such as we bear others. It is mingled with gratitude. And as we grow older, gratitude becomes the stronger feeling. And as gratitude assumes the supremacy, the feeling becomes sweeter and holier. It assumes a religious nature. It is baptized at the fountain of religion. And instead of glooming life, it because it is the power of love. "God is love." It is simple as the story of love in the human heart. "The wayfaring man, though a fool, need not err therein." All can easily learn how to love God. Ask the Saviour, and he will say, "Love thy Father." This is the burden of the glorious sermon of His life. If we love the Father, it must be in Christ. He has shown us the Father. Through no other name under heaven is the Father given. By no other can we come to the Father, for no other has shown him. Christ is the only way open. How simple, how beautiful—"Love thy Father, and thou shalt be saved"—saved from darkness and sin!

Christ is the same as God speaking to us; it is God through Christ saying, "Love me, and thou shalt be blest." It is as though a good father said to his child, "Love me, and thou shalt be a good and happy child." The child that loves the Father will obey the Father's voice of wisdom, and be good as he is great. Love of the parent is the seed of virtue. Love of God is the seed of religion. It is full of gratitude, humility, meekness; it is self-sacrificing, forbearing, merciful; burdened with the sweet spirit of forgiveness. The love of God is the central love sending out its influence through the whole heart and life. Who loves God is saved from hatred, impiety, from all intentional wrong. His heart is made the receptacle of a principle of eternal love, and hence of "eternal life." This love molds and modifies the character; checks the impulses; sways the passions; subdues enmity; elevates the affections; gives the ruling loves to truth, to heaven, makes it more cheerful and bright. It sweetens the whole heart and sheds a moral and affectionate influence through the whole mind.

Similar to this love of parents, and growing out of it, should be our love to God. Him we should regard as our parent. As such we should always think of Him. In all our works, and walks, and joys He should be present in our minds as our Father. Sweet shall be our thoughts of Him. Cheerfully should we meditate upon His wonderful works and ways. Gladly should our hearts praise Him and our souls commune with him. His commands should inspire us with holy delight. All our life should be made radiant with the inspiring thoughts of our Father. His matchless love and marvelous wisdom should make us feel like little children, happily yet adoringly and gratefully receiving the gifts of parental goodness. With such a love as this growing in our hearts and shining in our lives, how good and happy must we be! And yet this is religion. Love thy Father in heaven, is the full command. All else grows out of this. We can not love our fellows unless we love our Father. This is the sum of all Christ's teachings. He gave us the Father. "Show us the Father, and it sufficeth us." Before Christ, the Father was not known. God had only partially revealed himself. The glory of the full revelation was reserved for the immortal and immaculate Son. To know or love the Father is eternal life. This is the religion of the Saviour—this the religion of redemption. Salvation is in it. It is the power of God to God; gives its sanction to virtue; adorns the mind with the graces of godliness; sweetens the heart with amenities of goodness, and dignifies the soul with a spiritual assimilation to the Father. Man thus becomes a spiritual child of God. He is by a nature a natural child, and he is thus by grace or love made a spiritual child. Under the power of this love the world assumes a new aspect; it becomes a secondary object, good in its place, but only a means of spiritual improvement. Life becomes sublime in its great ends and eternal results. The soul of man becomes, at least in prospect, a glorious and eternal thing, often darkened by error and polluted by sin, but the object of God's love and care and the Redeemer's solicitude, progressively unfolding its powers and putting on its beauties under the sunshine of the All-seeing eye. And the race of men become the children of the great and loving Father, whose care and smiles no figures shall number, no ages wear out. This is the religion we believe the Saviour inculcated among men, which was the power of God unto salvation, the central and all-powerful idea of which is love. This is the religion in which thousands are this day rejoicing and living lives which are the brightest ornaments of humanity. And this is the religion which we offer to our youthful friends as the only cure for sin-sick humanity—the only safe guide through life—the only hope and strength of youth, manhood, and old age. We have not a separate religion for youth, nor a distinct religious life for them to live different from the old. It is the beauty of true religion, as of true love, that it lasts through all seasons. It is to grow by, live by, and die by ; and, what is more, to rise through endless ages by. We understand this to be an eternal religion. Who becomes truly religious here, learns so much of heaven, walks so far in the celestial road. A truthful, religious life is the first step *in* heaven, not *to* heaven. Christ calls it the kingdom of heaven. Without the principles of religious love no woman's character is perfect, or so perfect as it may be. However learned, refined, or cultured she may be by art and society, if her soul is not baptized in this religious love, this love of the Father, she lacks the most essential beauty of spiritual womanhood. If she is not grateful to God, not in love with his glorious perfections, she is yet low and worldly. Her soul is bound in the chains of sense. It is this religion which adds the finishing touch of excellency to woman's character. It is this which makes her divine. In her best estate she is only earthly till this has wrought its redeeming work within her. To be blessed as she may be to make her life good and spiritually grand, she should begin early this devotion to the Father. Her heart should in early youth turn its face to its God and look up in sweet and grateful adoration. Woman's heart is the natural shrine of religion ; and this shrine should be dedicated while she is young. In cheerful confidence she should give her soul to her Father in heaven. The earlier she does it, the truer and happier will be her life. It is a sad mistake that religion is depressing and saddening to youth. " It is the soul's calm sunshine and the heartfelt joy." It is good for youth as for old age—as good to rejoice as to mourn by. It is as much for sunshine as for shade. He who has the most of it is the lightest-hearted man.

It is as fitting for the marriage altar as for the burial scene. It is calculated as much to elevate and gladden the cheerful heart as to relieve and bless the sorrowful one. Woman in all her relations has an especial need of religion to sustain her. Her pathway is beset with trials. She loves and must love her friends. These, one after another, are separated from her by the customs or accidents of society, or the stern hand of death ; sickness and misfortune must come upon her. Her soul is sensitive, and she feels keenly the severing of love's dearest ties. Nowhere else can she find a balm for her aching heart but in the bosom of the Father. If her heart is spiritualized by a holy religious love, there will come to her ministering spirits in the hopes and joys of religion which will bring relief.

Oh, if I could impress on the young female mind the importance of this subject, I should do the world a benefit we could not estimate. Think of a woman all through life shedding about her the genial influence of true religion. From early youth to latest age she is an evangel of peace and love. Her steps are marked with deeds of charity ; her life is radiant with goodness. She loves her Father, and, loving him, she loves his children ; and, loving them, both her and her heart grow large and her soul strong and beautiful. Her life is a song of praise. Men love to do her secret homage, and in many a heart she is surnamed "angel."

Why should any woman think to live without religion? Oh, how sad is her life without it—how dark her death! It is only in religious love that the future becomes bright, and hope changes to cheerful faith. I have presented woman's religious duty in a simple form of love to God. I have not time to speak of its detail, nor the means of cultivating this love and growing in the Divine grace; these are given in the sublime yet simple words of Jesus of Nazareth. To him I refer you for light to guide you.

I wish to speak a little of an objection that often comes up to the view of the subject I have taken. It is this: "How can we love a being we have not seen? a Father we have not known? a God we can not comprehend?" The objection is a strong one in many minds, and for such I will show how it looks to me.

Our daily experience tells us that we can love beings we have never seen. I doubt not that every American loves Washington. His name is dear to us all. His character and life are our boast and admiration. Not more should we love him if we had seen him and known him well. It is his *character* that we have and not his person. His character is as clear and glorious to us as it was to his compeers. It thrills us as delightfully and moves upon us as powerfully as it did upon them. It is a glory hung around the name of America to which the world looks with a reverent and admiring joy. To tell me that I can not love Washington would be to rob me of the highest pride I feel in my country. I love him for what he was in the day of his earthly glory, the man of all majesty, the pride of all nations. I love him for what he did, for the life of spotless virtue and magnificent wisdom and goodness. He lived for the good of his country and the world. I love him for the tall angel of light that he now is, and the celestial richness of the glory that streams from his brow. I know I love him, and no philosophy or skepticism can cheat me out of that love.

I could name a hundred characters that have lived in the past and now live in heaven that I know I love in the same way. I love them as really as I do my personal friends, and love them in proportion to the greatness and goodness I see in them. I may say the same of many living men and women. Speaking from my own experience, I should say that I can love goodness, worth, all that is lovable in character as well as in a being that I have not seen as one that I have. I have known of people who have an earthly father living that they have never seen, and whom they love with a deep and rich fervency of affection. I have known of children whom poverty or accident has separated in infancy from their mother, and who cherished for that unknown, far-off maternal friend a sacred and deathless love. They have meditated hours, days, and weeks on the sad separation and the sweet, holy bosom from which they drew the breath of life. In well-formed minds this love grows up with their growth and strengthens with their strength. The idea of parentage awakens love in the heart. The relation is so near and dear it can not be otherwise in good and cultured minds. Then we can love a father whom we have not seen. We all know that the idea of God is a spontaneity in the human mind. Though God may be incomprehensible and his ways past finding out, he is still so much within and around us that we can not keep the thoughts of him out of our minds. We know, too, that thousands do love Him with a deathless love who can comprehend him no better than we. We may infer from this that we can love Him also.

But when we think of His character, its infinite loveliness, its unfathomable depth of love, and wisdom, and holiness, it seems to me that the impossibility is in not loving him. How can we help loving him? Add to this that He is our Father, out of the depth of whose being we were born, and that he loves us with an unspeakable and eternal love, and the attraction to love him becomes still stronger. Then think how much He has done for us; how he has given us our parents and friends, and all the dear and delightful objects of life, thought, and hope; and more than this, has given us Jesus, and with him the glorious Gospel, revealing an immortal life and a glorious inheritance beyond the Jordan of death. These benefactions of His love make his character appear infinitely attractive, so that the wonder would seem to be that any should fail to love him.

It seems clear that the Father may be none the less loved on account of his being unseen. We are constituted to love things unseen. And if we scan it closely we shall find that we really love nothing else. Character worth, virtue, goodness, love, wisdom, knowledge, science, philosophy, religion, are all unseen. So the charm about a person that makes us love him is unseen. Indeed, it is the unseen we love, and nothing else. We are spiritual beings, and made for spiritual exercises. Our nature is exactly adapted to the love and worship of an unseen God. When we do not do it we are acting contrary to our nature. We deny ourselves as well as God when we do not love and adore him. Is it proper for youth to do so? By no means. All youth, and especially young women, should feel that so long as they neglect their religious duties they neglect the most important concerns of their eternal existence. They are not ephemeral, but eternal creatures. Their relation to God and each other are eternal ones. They are on the sea of being—turn back they can not. God is above and around them, and always will be. The sooner they love Him, the better it will be for them. To love Him is spiritual life; to love him not is death.

It is a glorious thing to live life well. They can not do it without religion. Woman is scarcely woman unless the great principle of love guides her. That principle, directed toward God and man, is the sum total of the Christian religion. Let every young woman so direct it that her whole life may be radiant with the light and deeds of love.

Lecture Thirteen.

WOMANHOOD.

Woman not an Adornment only—Civilization Elevates Woman—Woman not what She should be—Woman's Influence Over-rated—Force of Character Necessary—The Virtue of True Womanhood—Passion is not always Love—True Love is only for Worth—Good Behavior and Deportment—Spiritual Harmony Desirable—Importance of Self-control—What shall Woman do?—Strive to be a True Woman.

WHAT is womanhood? Is there any more important question for young women to consider than this? It should be the highest ambition of every young woman to possess a true womanhood. Earth presents no higher object of attainment. To be a woman, in the truest and highest sense of the word, is to be the best thing beneath the skies. To be a woman is something more than to live eighteen or twenty years; something more than to grow to the physical stature of women; something more than to wear flounces, exhibit drygoods, sport jewelry, catch the gaze of lewd-eyed men; something more than to be a belle, a wife, or a mother. Put all these qualifications together, and they do but little toward making a true woman. A true woman exists independent of outward attachments. It is not wealth, or beauty of person, or connection, or station, or power of mind, or literary attainments, or variety and richness of outward accomplishments, that make the woman. These often adorn womanhood as the ivy adorns the oak. But they should never be mistaken for the thing they adorn. This is the grand error of womankind. They take the shadow for the substance—the glitter for the gold—the heraldry and trappings of the world for the priceless essence of womanly worth which exists within the mind. Here is where almost the whole world has erred. Woman has been regarded as an adornment. Because God has conferred upon her the charm of a beauty not elsewhere found in earth, the world has vainly imagined she was made to glory in its exhibition. Hence woman is too often a vain, idle, useless thing. She stoops to be the plaything of man, the idol of his vanity, the victim of his lust. In stooping, she lays off her womanhood to pander to the low aims of a sensual life. In every country and in all ages woman has been thus abased. The history of the world is all darkened by the awful shadow of woman's debasement. While man has admired and loved her, he has degraded her. Savage and civilized man are not very dissimilar in this respect. They both woo, cajole, and flatter woman to oppress and degrade her. They both load her with honeyed titles and flattering compliments, as though to sweeten with sugar-plum nonsense her bitter pressure of wrongs. It is the consent of all historians that woman has been elevated in proportion as knowledge and virtue have advanced among mankind. No one can read the history of the world without seeing that woman is upward bound. No one can look at woman's present estate, her devotion to vanity, her meagre knowledge, her narrow culture, her circumscribed sphere of action, her monotonous and aimless life, without feeling that she has many long steps yet to take before she will attain to her true position, her full womanhood. I would not intimate that man's love for woman is not sincere, nor that he designs any harm to her. Nor would I intimate that woman purposely stoops to degrade herself. The Indian loves his dusky maid with a deep sincerity of heart; but that love does not prevent him from acquiescing in the common custom of his people, and making her his drudge, and regarding her as his inferior and his life-bound slave. So the civilized man loves his wife with an ardency of devotion he feels for no other object; but that does not prevent him from subjecting her to the common lot of woman, or from believing it right that woman should be deprived by custom and law of that culture, those stimulants, and privileges, and rights which belong to her as an accountable being Civilized men do not demand that their women shall be trained to the highest culture—shall be taught in the deepest wisdom—shall live for the broadest and grandest purposes. No; they think it is enough if their women can have a little smattering of knowledge so as to appear well in the drawing-room parlor. Wisdom is for men. Man alone may draw from the *deep* wells of knowledge. Why have civilized men closed all their colleges and universities against women? Why have they shut almost every avenue to public usefulness, to honorable distinction, to virtuous endeavor, against woman? Why have they deprived her of power, and compelled her to submit to man in all the relations of life? It is not for the want of a sincere love for her. No; it is rather for a want of an enlightened view of what woman should be. Men, as well as women, have failed to comprehend the true idea of womanhood. Both have been satisfied with too little in woman. They have borne with the narrowness of woman's culture and the aimlessness of her life, believing it all right. It is a fact—a glaring, solemn, humiliating fact—that woman is not what she should be. She is weak, thoughtless, heartless, compared with what she should be. Look at the world. Woman is said to be mistress of her home. The mother is called the maker of her children's characters. Is it so? See the drunkards, tipplers, tobacco-mongers, libertines, gamblers, swearers, brawlers, robbers, murderers. There is a great army of them. They all constitute a large share of the men and some of the women of our world. Where are the mothers who will acknowledge that they made the characters of these people? Where are the mothers who teach their boys to chew, and smoke, and swear? to drink, and brawl, and fight? to do those deeds of darkness which the sun refuses to shine upon? Somebody has taught them these things. If their mothers did not, who did? If their mothers had been wise and forcible, as they should have been, would the children have been so easily led astray? If women had that influence which some attribute to them, would these things be so?

If they had the influence they ought to have, would they be so? Talk as we will about woman's influence, it is not what it should be. We all know that if woman ruled the world, she would have less low, drunken, rowdy, sensual men. It has long been a hollow compliment which man has paid to woman to tell her that she rules the world. But no man believes it when he says it. Every woman should spurn the compliment as slanderous. Woman would rule the world better if it was under her control. Why are so many young men reckless, drunken, profane, and lawless? It is not because young women would have them so. Far from it. Their female associates do not hold half the control over them that they ought.

Young women ought to hold a steady moral sway over their male associates, so strong as to prevent them from becoming such lawless rowdies. Why do they not? Because they do not possess sufficient *force* of character. They have not sufficient resolution and energy of purpose. Their virtue is not vigorous. Their moral wills are not resolute. Their influence is not armed with executive power. Their goodness is not felt as an earnest force of benevolent purpose. Their moral convictions are not regarded as solemn resolves to be true to God and duty, come what may. Their opinions are not esteemed as the utterances of wisdom. Their love is not accepted as the strong purpose of a devout soul to be true to its highest ideas of affectionate life. In no particular do they make impressions of strong moral force. They do not exert the deep, resistless influence of full-grown womanhood.' The great lack of young women is a lack of *power*. They do not make themselves felt. They need more force of character. It is not enough that they are *pure*. They must be virtuous; that is, they must possess that virtue which wins laurels in the face of temptation; which is backed by a mighty force of moral principle; which frowns on evil with a rebuking authority; which will not compromise its dignity, nor barter its prerogatives for the gold or fame of the world, the very frown of which would annihilate him who would attempt to seduce it; which claims as its right such virtue in its associates. There is a virtue which commands respect; which awes by its dignity and strength; a virtue exhibited in such commanding strength of moral purpose as silences every vile wish to degrade it; a virtue that knows why it hates evil, why it loves right, why it cleaves to principle as to life; a virtue more mighty in its potency than any other force—which gives a sublime grandeur to the soul in which it dwells and the life it inspires. This is the virtue that belongs to womanhood. It is the virtue every young woman should possess. It is not enough to have an easy kind of virtue which more than half courts temptation; which is pure more from a fear of society's rebuke than a love of right; which rebukes sin so faintly that the sinner feels encouraged to proceed; which smiles on small offenses, and kindly fondles the pet evils of society out of which in the end grow the monsters. This is the virtue of too many women.

They would not have a drunkard for a husband, but they would drink a glass of wine with a fast young man. They would not use profane language, but they are not shocked by its incipient language, and love the society of men whom they know are as profane as Lucifer out of their presence. They would not be dishonest, but they will use a thousand deceitful words and ways, and countenance the society of men known as hawkers, sharpers, and deceivers. They would not be irreligious, but they smile upon the most irreligious men, and even show that they love to be wooed by them. They would not be licentious, but they have no stunning rebuke for licentious men, and will even admit them on parol into their society. This is the virtue of too many women—a virtue scarcely worthy the name—really no virtue at all—a milk-and-water substitute—a hypocritical, hollow pretension to virtue as unwomanly as it is disgraceful. This is not the virtue of true womanhood. Do young women propose for themselves the strong virtue of womanhood, which is an impregnable fortress of righteous principle? If not, they should do it. It should be their first work to conceive the idea of such a virtuous principle as an indwelling life, and when conceived it should be sought as the richest wealth, as the grandest human attainment—as that alone which confers upon woman a divine grace.

Nor is it enough that young women *love* well. To be on fire of an adulterous love or a blind passion, which is little better, is one thing; and to love righteously, nobly, steadily, is another thing. Woman naturally has great strength of affection. She loves by an irresistible impulse. But that love is not worthy unless it be directed to worthy objects and swayed by high moral principles. The love of a woman should be as the love of an angel. It should swell in her bosom as a great tide of moral life, binding her to beauty of soul, worth of character, excellency of life. She should not waste her love on unworthy objects, on impure and lecherous men or women. Her love, to be truly womanly, must not be a love of person or outward charms, so much as a love of principle, a love of magnanimity, integrity, wisdom, affection, piety; a love of whatever may magnify and adorn a human soul. It is unwomanly to waste the high energies of her love on the material charms of an elegant person, or the brilliant accomplishments of cultured manners, unless they are united with true worth of character. The love of womanhood is the love of worth, the love of mental harmony and spiritual powers. True, woman may pity corruption, may sympathize with all manner of offenders; may give the force of her compassion to the erring and unrighteous; so she may admire genius, culture, the beauty of person, and the charms of manner; but her love is only for real worth, for that which is enduring and Godlike. She may find pleasure in many things and persons that she must not, can not love. Love is too precious to be wasted on any thing but its legitimate objects, wealth of mind and worth of character.

Nor yet is it enough that young women *behave* well. Something more is needed than a correct outward life.

Many behave well who have but little worth of character They behave well because it is best for their social standing—because society loves good behavior and pays it the compliment of respect. It is well to behave well. There is no true life without becoming behavior. We have all praise for good behavior. It should be one great object in every young woman's life to study for a becoming and womanly behavior. Her manners should be agreeable; her conversation should be chaste and proper; her deportment should be dignified and easy; her regard for propriety and fitness in all she says and does should be made manifest; and in all respects her behavior should be such as becomes womanhood. But while we recommend this as of very great importance, we say it is not enough. Good behavior must spring from a good heart. If it is studied as an outside fitness, a cloak, or a fashionable attire, it will not answer the purpose for which it is intended. A purely outside life is a sham, and sooner or later defeats itself. There is no concealing a bad heart. It may be done for a little while, but it can not be kept concealed. Like murder, it will out. So a heart that is not particularly bad, but only lacks true principle, will soon expose its hollowness. Its want of moral power will be felt. But even if it would not expose itself, it would be infinitely best to imbue it with righteous principle. For itself, for its own happiness, it must be good.

Genuine good behavior springs from an inward harmony of character which blends all inward essences of good. It does not come from any one, nor a few great virtues. It is the mingled result of all. Young women, then, must not be satisfied with possessing a few good traits of character. They must strive for all; for it is only in the possession of all that inward harmony can be enjoyed. The beauty of woman's life grows out of this harmony. A mind jarred by inward discord can never ultimate a good life. This discord will show itself in the life. Spiritual harmony is the great attainment all should have in view. In this lies the charm of womanhood. Out from this goes the sweet influences of the outward life. The divine grace of womanly propriety is the fruit that grows from this combination of all excellences.

To attain this, the first thing is self-control. How few women have any thing like a respectable amount of self-control. The great majority are nervous, excitable, fidgety. They frighten at a spider, laugh at a silly joke, love at first sight, go into spasms at disappointment, cry about trifles, have a fit of admiration at the sight of a pretty dress, have as many moods in a day as the wind, and in all respects exhibit every indication of the most disorderly, uncontrolled mind. Talk about harmony in such a character! We may as well look for wisdom in the house of folly. No mental habit is worse than that of giving the reins to our impulses. They are sure to lead us into difficulty. There is scarcely a more disgusting sight than a woman, well endowed, all given up to the sway of her impulses. Trust her! Why, you may as well trust the wind. Love her! You may as well fix your affections on the vanishing rainbow. Hope for good at her hands! As well hope for stability among the clouds. A useless, dangerous, troublesome, miserable thing is a woman of impulse. And yet there are thousands of them. They keep themselves and the world in a grand effervescence. If there is any evil to be avoided, it is this. If there is any virtue to be sought, it is self-control. And yet it is difficult of attainment in our order of society. Women are so shut up from healthy air and exercise, so excluded from ennobling avocations, so hemmed in by conventional rules, so compelled to have waiters, assistants, beaux, somebody to lead them, advise them, do for them, think for them—are so annoyed by petty cares and trifling vexations, and so subjected to abuses, both of a private and public nature, that self-control is a virtue harder of attainment than almost any other. Yet none is needed more than this. And it must be attained, or the glory of womanhood can never be put on. If the struggle is hard, the victory will be all the grander. Let no young woman give up in despair. The power is in her if she will but use it. She may be the queen of her own soul if she will. All depends upon the force of her will.

Young women have much to hope for, and the world much to hope for at their hands. A better idea of womanhood is growing up in the minds of men. Woman's wrong, difficulties, and trials are being felt. Her aimless, hopeless life is being mourned over. The evils from a false society preying upon all womankind are being felt;

and almost every woman is beginning to feel the approaching indications of a better time coming. Women are asking, "What shall we do? We wish not to be idle. We feel too much shut out from useful avocations. We feel too little opportunity to work out for ourselves such characters as we know we ought to possess. We must, we will do something for our own elevation."

Let every young woman determine to do something for the honor and elevation of her sex. At least let her determine that she will possess and always wear about her as her richest possession a true womanhood. This is the most that she can do. Above all, let her not throw obstacles in the way of her sisters, who are striving nobly to be useful, but rather help them with the weight of her encouragement and counsel. Let her determine that for herself she will do her own thinking; that she will form her own opinions from her own investigations; that she will persist in holding the highest principles of womanly morality and the virtuous attainments which constitute a true womanhood. When she has done this, let her call to her aid all the force of character she can command to enable her to persist in being a woman of the true stamp. In every class of society the young women should awake to their duty. They have a great work to do. It is not enough that they should be what their mothers were. They must be more. The spirit of the times calls on woman for a higher order of character and life. Will young women heed the call? Will they emancipate themselves from the fetters of custom and fashion, and come up a glorious company to the possession of a vigorous, virtuous, noble womanhood—a womanhood that shall shed new light upon the world, and point the way to a divine life? We wait to hear the answer in the coming order of women.

Lecture Fourteen.

HAPPINESS.

Happiness Desired—Fretful People—Motes in the Eye—We were Made for Happiness—Sorrow has Useful Lessons—Happiness a Duty—Despondency is Irreligious—Pleasure not always Happiness—The Misuse of the World—Contentment necessary to Happiness—Happiness must be sought aright—Truly seeking we shall Find—Our Success not always Essential—Happiness often Found Unexpectedly—Happiness overcomes Circumstances—A Tendency to Murmuring—God Rules over All—Health necessary to Happiness—Disease is Sinful—God Loves a Happy Soul—Happiness Possible to All.

It is commonly believed that men are nappy or unhappy according to circumstances. But this may well be questioned; for multitudes are intensely miserable under circumstances highly favorable to Happiness. The high-born, the wealthy, the distinguished, and even the good, are often unhappy. Many very excellent persons, whose lives are honorable and whose characters are noble, pass numberless hours of sadness and weariness of heart. The fault is not with their circumstances, nor yet with their general characters, but with themselves, that they are miserable. They have failed to adopt the true philosophy of life. They wait for Happiness to come instead of going to work and making it; and while they wait they torment themselves with borrowed troubles, with fears, forebodings, morbid fancies and moody spirits, till they are all unfitted for Happiness under any circumstances. Sometimes they cherish unchaste ambition, covet some fancies or real good which they do not deserve and could not enjoy if it were theirs, wealth they have not earned, honors they have not won, attentions they have not merited, love which their selfishness only craves. Sometimes they undervalue the good they do possess ; throw away the pearls in hand for some beyond their reach, and often less valuable ; trample the flowers about them under their feet ; long for some never seen, but only heard or read of ; and forget present duties and joys in future and far-off visions. Sometimes they shade the present with every cloud of the past, and although surrounded by a thousand inviting duties and pleasures, revel in sad memories with a kind of morbid relish for the stimulus of their miseries. Sometimes, forgetting the past and present, they live in the future, not in its probable realities, but in its most improbable visions and unreal creations, now of good and then of evil, wholly unfitting their minds for real life and enjoyments. These morbid and improper states of mind are too prevalent among young women. They excite that nervous irritability which is so productive of pining regrets and fretful complaints. They make that large class of fretters who enjoy no peace themselves, nor permit others to about them. In the domestic circle they fret their life away. Every thing goes wrong with them because they make it so. The smallest annoyances chafe them as though they were unbearable aggravations. Their business and duties trouble them as though such things were not good. Pleasure they never seem to know because they never get ready to enjoy it. Even the common movements of Providence are all wrong with them. The weather is never as it should be. The seasons roll on badly. The sun is never properly tempered. The climate is always charged with a multitude of vices. The winds are everlastingly perverse, either too high or too low, blowing dust in everybody's face, or not fanning them as they should. The earth is ever out of humor, too dry or too wet, too muddy or dusty. And the people are just about like it. Something is wrong all the time, and the wrong is always just about them. Their home is the worst of anybody's; their street and their neighborhood is the most unpleasant to be found; nobody else has so bad servants and so many annoyances as they. Their lot is harder than falls to common mortals; they have to work harder and always did; have less and always expect to. They have seen more trouble than other folks know any thing about. They are never so well as their neighbors, and they always charge all their unhappiness upon those nearest connected with them, never dreaming that they are themselves the authors of it all. Such people are to be pitied. Of all the people in the world they deserve most our compassion. They are good people in many respects, very benevolent, very conscientious, very pious, but, withal, very annoying to themselves and others. As a general rule, their goodness makes them more difficult to cure of their evil. They can not be led to see that they are at fault. Knowing their virtues they can not see their faults. They do not perhaps over-estimate their virtues, but fail to see what they lack, and what they lack they charge upon others, often upon those who love them best. They see others' actions through the shadow of their own fretful and gloomy spirits. Hence it is that they see their own faults as existing in those about them, as a defect in the eye produces the appearance of a corresponding defect in every object toward which it is turned. This defect in character is more generally the result of vicious or improper habits of mind, than any constitutional idiosyncrasy. It is the result of the indulgence of gloomy thoughts, morbid fancies, inordinate ambition, habitual melancholy, a complaining, fault-finding disposition. It is generally early acquired, not in childhood, but in youth. Childhood is too buoyant, fresh, and free for such indulgences. Early youth—when its passions are developing, when the soul's bubbling springs are opening fresh and warm, when young hopes put out, to be blighted with a shade, young loves come to be disappointed with a frown, young desires aspire to be saddened with the first failure—is the season when the seeds of disquiet and unhappiness are sown in the soul. And in the most gifted and sensitive souls these seeds are oftenest sown. Those of highly poetic temperaments, of delicate and almost divine psychology, in whom some little constitutional unbalance existed at the beginning of life, and whose judgments developed slower than their passions, are often those who drink the bitterest waters of life. Beautiful souls, sitting in the shadow of self-gathered clouds! We pity and love them. We never see one without longing to bless it. Oh, could they but know how unbecoming such powers and virtues are, such gloominess and disquiet, they would rouse themselves to the glories of a morning life, and, shaking the dews of the night from their wings, would soar aloft in the sunshine of wisdom and love. Having tasted the bitter waters of sorrow, they may appreciate, perhaps all the better, the sweet nectar of life which ought to flow from all our states of mind and outward actions. We were not made for sorrow, but for joy. Our souls were not so delicately wrought to be wasted in fear and melancholy. Our minds were not so gifted to spend themselves on clouds and in darkness. Our hearts were not so firmly strung to wail notes of grief and woe. This beautiful world, so ever fresh and new about us, was not designed to imprison self-convicted souls away from its sunshine and flowers. The bending heavens arching so grandly over us, so studded with sparkling joy-lights, and animated with the eternal cotillion of the skies, invites to no such irreverent repining. Creation's wide field of animated existence inspires no such moodiness and fretfulness of spirit. It is all wrong; it is absolutely sinful. We have no moral right to make ourselves or others so unhappy. We were made for happiness as well as holiness. All life's duties and experiences, when properly understood, are the steps that lead tc the temple of eternal good. Disappointments and crosses may come, but let them come; they bring their lessons of wisdom.

Failures may crush our hopes and stop us on life's way; but we may gather up and go on again rejoicing in what we have learned. Toils may demand our time and energies; let us give them; labor creates strength and imparts knowledge. Others may use our earnings, and require our care and support; let it be so: "It is more blessed to give than to receive."

Our friends may die and leave our hearts and homes desolate for a time; we can not prevent it, nor would it be best if we could. Sorrow has its useful lessons when it is legitimate, and death is the gate that opens out of earth toward the house "eternal in the heavens." If we lose them, heaven gains them. If we mourn, they rejoice. If we hang our harps on the willows, they tune theirs in the eternal orchestra above, rejoicing that we shall soon be with them. Shall we not drown our sorrow in the flood of light let through the rent vail of the skies which Jesus entered, and, to cure our loneliness, gather to us other friends to walk life's way, knowing that every step brings us nearer the departed, and their sweet, eternal home, which death never enters, and where partings are never known? We may still love the departed. They are ours as ever, and we are theirs. The ties that unite us are not broken. They are too strong for death's stroke. They are made for the joys of eternal friendship. Other friendships on earth will not disturb these bonds that link with dear ones on high. Nor will our duties below interfere with the sacredness of our relations with them. They wish not to see us in sorrow. They doubtless sympathize with us; and could we hear their sweet voices, they would tell us to dry our tears, and bind ourselves to other friends, and joyfully perform all duties on earth till our time to ascend shall come.

Every lesson of life, wisely read, tells us that we should be happy; that we should seek to be happy from principle, not simply from impulse; that we should make Happiness a great object in life; that our duties, our varied relations to our fellows as friends, as lovers, as companions, as parents, as children; our avocations, our labors, sacrifices, hopes, trials, struggles, should administer to our Happiness. And it is our business to see that they do. Is it a duty to be good? It is just as much a duty to be happy, to train our minds to pleasant moods, and our hearts to cheerful feelings. There is no duty more sanctioned by every moral obligation than the duty to be happy. We have no moral right to make others miserable, or to permit them to remain so when we can help it. No more right have we to torment our own souls, or to permit habitual sadness and despondency to weigh down our spirits. It is well for every young person to seek true moral light upon this subject; and especially for young women, for their peculiarly sensitive and affectionate nature, their confined habits and employments, their cares multiplying as they grow older, and their body-wearying and soul-trying experiences and labors demand the very best philosophy and religion of life; and more so as the men with whom their lots will be likely to be cast appreciate so little the trials and experiences of woman's life. They ought to start out resolutely determined to be happy, to seek the good of every thing. This should be the first precept in their moral mode, the first article in their creed, the first resolution demanded by their religion. We have no confidence in a gloomy religion. Human souls were never made to do penance, to lacerate and torment themselves in worship or duty. Every truth in the theology of the Bible beams with a glory that ought to illuminate our minds with a light almost divine. Every principle of "the glorious Gospel of the blessed God" is benignant and smiling with the love of the Father, and ought to animate our souls with the joy of a steady blessedness. Every duty demanded by the Christian religion is but the requirement of perfect love, and should quicken our consciences to the most lively satisfaction. To be desponding and gloomy is indeed irreligious. Hearty joy is the fruit of religion. Swelling gladness is the praise-note of the truly Christian spirit. There are no possessions like religious possessions to fill the soul with true enjoyment. And what are they? They are, first: a mind in harmony with the works and ways of God, which sees the Father in the daily movements of the spheres and the providential arrangements of the world; in the blossoming life of spring, and the withered death of winter; in the dear relations of domestic life, and the more showy fraternities of nations; in birth, and life, and death; in every provision for happiness found in the wide range of the physical and spiritual universe; secondly, a conscience void of offense toward God and man; in love with right, bound to righteous principle in a wedlock that knows no breaking; devout, honest, kind, because it is right and Godlike so to be; which rules the mind and life with a gentle but powerful sway, leading where angels walk in every pure and honest word and work; and thirdly, a heart swelling with love to God and man; an earnest, warm, good-willing heart, lighting its face with sunshine, and softening its hand with tenderness; a heart that can melt in others' woes, and glow in others' joys, pure and chaste, subdued and calm. Such a mind, such a conscience, such a heart afford true religious enjoyments. The more one has of such possessions, the happier he must be. With such a mind, the true philosophy of life is clear—it is that we were made to be happy in righteousness and truth, and should bend all our energies to guard our hearts from every fretful and desponding feeling, and make every experience in life bless and make us happy. Oh, young woman! set your heart on Happiness; not on pleasure that floats on the surface of life, but on that inward peace that dwells in the soul devoted to all good. The things about us are designed to administer to our Happiness, and we should *use* them for this purpose. The world we live in is for our use. Food, raiment, money, wealth are for use. They are adapted to good ends in life. They help us to comfort, convenience, beauty, and knowledge. Wisely used, they serve us well; but abused, they sting us with many poisoned darts. The most of us make ourselves miserable by a misuse of the world. We fret our souls well-nigh to death about dress, food, houses, lands, goods, wealth. We live for these things, as though serving them could give us Happiness. We are ambitious of gains and gold, as though these could answer the soul's great wants, as though these could think and love, admire and worship. We chase the illusive glitter of fashion as though it was a crown of glory, and could impart dignity and peace to its wearer. We hunt after pleasure as though it could be found by searching. Pleasure comes of itself. It must never be wooed. She is a coy maid, and ever eludes her flattering followers. She will come and abide with us when we use wisely the world and its good things. But we must put things to their true use, else pleasure will keep away. Oh, how much might we enjoy life if we would put things to their true use! When the sun shines, we must love it and think of its treasures of wealth to the world. When the cloud rises, we must admire its somber glory, for it is big with blessings. The morning must be accepted as a rosy blessing, the evening as a quiet prelude to repose; the day as an opportunity for achievements worthy of us, and the night for refreshing rest and recruit.

Our friends we must prize and appreciate while we are with them. It is a shame not to know how much we love our friends, and how good they are till they die. We must seize with joy all our opportunities; our duties we must perform with pleasure; our sacrifices we must make cheerfully, knowing that he who sacrifices most is noblest; we must forgive with an understanding of the glory of forgiveness, and use the blessings we have, realizing how great are small blessings when properly accepted. I have known men sit to a table comfortably spread with wholesome food and make themselves and all with them miserable because it lacked something their pampered palate craved. A true man will *enjoy* a crust of bread, and if he has nothing more, count it a God-send that may save his life. I have seen women embroil a comfortable home with constant disquiet because it was not so grand as their vanity desired; and others never tire in their complaints against a very good house because it was destitute of a convenience or two that some other house had. I have seen young women completely miserable because some article of dress did not harmonize with the last fashioned plait, or some of their surroundings were not quite so beautiful or agreeable as those of some wealthier friend. Forgetting to use what they had to administer to their Happiness, they tormented their souls because they had not something else. All these repinings and complaints come from unchaste spirits. Wisdom dwells not in such souls. The little we have we should enjoy, and if we need or wish more we should labor cheerfully to obtain it, and rejoice in our labor and hope. We should seek to draw Happiness from every little incident in life, from every thing we have, and every thing by which we are surrounded. This is the secret of much Happiness. I believe all desire to be happy. It seems to be the one great wish of the human soul in which all the others center. But desire is not enough. We must seek the Happiness we wish; seek it in the wisdom which opens life's mysteries plainly to our view; which reveals our present and eternal relations, and points out the ways of pleasantness and peace. Would we know the *truth*, the gemmy walks of knowledge, the flowery bowers of inward and joyous life, the teachings of nature, revelation, the Son and the Father? We must seek, else how shall we find them? These things do not come of themselves. Our minds do not develop truth as the forest develops leaves or the prairie flowers, without effort. Truth is without, and must be sought. Would we find the path of *duty?* We must seek it in earnest effort to find and enjoy. And we must seek it with a full determination to enjoy it when so found. We may seek gold, honor, worldly pleasures, and not enjoy them when we find them, because we do not seek them in the right spirit, with an enlightened view of their uses and a determination to enjoy them in those uses. So we may seek Gospel riches, divine light, the instructions of the Word, and find much for which we seek, and be but little benefited because we have not resolved to be guided by the light we find and blessed by its divine spirit. If we would be happy, then, we must *seek* to be happy, not without the use of proper and ordained means—not without a thorough consecration of our souls to the good of what we seek, but with a resolute will and determination in the use of all proper means to mold our spirits into the best and happiest moods.

We must seek Happiness in the ways in which it is to be found, in study, duty, labor, improving pleasure, with a constant inward effort to find it, to make it out of what we find. We must seek it in domestic and business life; in the relations we hold to our fellow-men; in the opportunities for discipline, self-sacrifice, forgiveness, resistance of temptation; in the changes and vicissitudes of life; in nature, revelation, ourselves, and God. If we thus seek, we shall find. This is the promise, and thousands have realized it. It is not a promise for the future world only, but for this also. We have the promise of this world as well as that which is to come. We need not wait for the golden gate to open to be as happy as our capacity will admit. We may be happy here. Happiness is not hid away beyond our search, nor laid above our reach, nor reserved for the spirit-world. We may enjoy this life and its holy relations. Our hearts, our homes, our lives may all glow with Happiness on earth. The means for it are all in our hands. The opportunities are daily open to us. In the dear amenities of home and its dulcet loves; in the elevating pleasures of society; in the instructing pursuits of science, duty, and daily life; in the cultivation of every personal virtue and every Gospel grace, we may enjoy in this life a sweet antepast of heaven. Only put forth the effort in the right way and the happy result will be ours.

But we must not be too dictatorial as to how we enjoy

life. We must not be too positive as to the manner in which we must find Happiness. We must not determine that it must come in just the way we wish, or else we will be miserable in the grief of disappointment. It is not for man wholly to direct his steps. Sometimes what he thinks for his good, turns out ill; and what he thinks a great evil, develops a great blessing in disguise. It is folly, almost madness, to be miserable because things are not as we would have them, or because we are disappointed in our plans. Many of our plans must be defeated. A multitude of little hopes must every day be crushed, and now and then a great one. Besides, the success of our plans is not always essential to our best interests or our Happiness. Sometimes success is our misery. Our plans are often our idols, to worship which is false and wrong. It is not in this, or that, or the other peculiar mode of life, nor in any particular class of outward circumstances; nor in any definite kind of labor, or duty, or pleasure, that we must look positively for Happiness; nor yet in any chosen place or society, or surroundings, or under any particular class of influences. If we do, we shall be disappointed; for it is not in our power to have things just our way, or to control our outward or associational life just as we would. We live amid a multitude of influences we can not altogether control. Nor is it best we should. Our vanity, or ignorance, or selfishness might do us great spiritual injury. We might soon become like spoiled children, or nerveless drones, or pampered aristocrats. What we are to control is ourselves, our minds. We must seek Happiness in the right state of mind, in the legitimate labors, duties, and pleasures of life, and then we shall find what we seek; yet we may often find it under very different circumstances from what we expected. We may look for it in one pursuit and find it in another; and sometimes where we expect the least we shall find the most; and where we look for the most we shall find the least. "The first shall be last and the last first." We are short-sighted, and fail to see the end of things. There is not a little of the misery of life comes from this disposition to have things our own way, as though we could not be happy under any circumstances only just those we have framed to suit our minds. Circumstances are not half so essential to our Happiness as most people imagine. A cabin is often the theater of more true Happiness than a palace. The dunghill as often enthrones the true philosophy of life as the seats which kings occupy. Women in humble circumstances often possess richer minds, sweeter hearts, a nobler and profounder peace than those of magnificent surroundings. The disposition to make the best of life is what we want to make us happy Those who are so willful and seemingly perverse about their outward circumstances, are often intensely affected by the merest trifles. A little thing shadows their life for days. The want of some little convenience, some personal gratification, some outward form or ornament, will blight a day's joy. They can often bear a great calamity better than a small disappointment, because they nerve themselves to meet the former, and yield to the latter without an effort to resist. Mole-hills are magnified into mountains, and in the shadow of these mountains they sit down and weep. The very things they ought to have sometimes come unasked, and because they are not ready for them, they will not enjoy them, but rather make them the causes of misery. There is a disposition also in such minds to multiply their troubles as well as magnify them. They make troubles of many things which should really be regarded as privileges, opportunities for self-sacrifice, for culture, for improving effort. They make troubles of the ordinary allotments of life, its duties, charities, changes, unavoidable accidents, reverses, and experiences. All this can be considered in no other light than morally wrong, for these common allotments and experiences were beyond all question ordained by Infinite Wisdom as a most healthy discipline for both the body and mind of man. All such complaining is ingratitude, practical impiety.

Nearly all people have their secret repinings, their unexpressed disquietude, because things are not as they would have them; because they do not possess some fancied good, or do experience some fancied misfortune. There is a tendency in all our minds to such inward murmurings. And this is wrong, and when we indulge in it, it is wicked. We ought not to make idols of our plans. We ought not to have too great attachments to our own ideas of what we must have, to be happy. If we do, we shall be very miserable, while we believe we are very good. The trouble is, we are too selfish, too unyielding in our arrangements for life's best good. Because we can not find Happiness in our own way, we will not accept it in any way, and so make ourselves miserable. I have known many very excellent people very unhappy from a kind of stubborn adherence to their settled convictions of just what they must have, how they must live, and what they must do to be happy. They lose sight of the fact that God rules above them, and a thousand influences work around them, partly, at least, beyond their control. They have not determined to accept life cheerfully in whatever form it may come, and seek for good—the "soul's calm sunshine and heartfelt joy"—under all circumstances, believing that all things work together for good to those who truly seek a divine life.

He who seeks a divine life and its pleasantness and peace in the right spirit, humble, earnest, loving, and cheerful, full of faith and hope, will realize that all things work together for his good. He may engage in life's duties and pleasures in the fullest confidence of this. Even his trials and disappointments will discipline his mind for noblest joys in store. They will work out good for his soul, which he will bear with him in life, and through the gate of death, as his crown and treasure above.

Thus far in the pursuit of this subject I have not considered Happiness as possible to a cold, selfish, worldly heart. One's aims must be good, or he can not expect inward peace. The Bible promises no peace to the wicked while he remains wicked. I am not authorized to promise any except to the righteous. Our hopes of Happiness for this world and the future must be founded in inward righteousness.

Now it really seems to me that nothing is more wanted among young women than a sound philosophy of life, one that they can live by and be happy in. Their duties and trials are to be great. Their influences are to strike into the hearts of the whole world. The generations to come are to be born of them. It is folly for them to expect to be happy by mere impulse. They must seek the Happiness of principle. They must make Happiness an object, and seek it with the use of all right means.

One consideration more is worthy of a moment's notice. It relates to health, both bodily and spiritual. One essential of health is cheerfulness of spirits. The weaknesses and diseases among females is most fearful. Only here and there is a healthy woman. And we attribute it in part to the great unrest and unspoken melancholy brooding in the great woman-soul of the world. Few, perhaps, fully realize the fearful truth of this remark. Many a beautiful woman is pining under a gloom she seldom expresses, and not more than half understands. Woman's confined life and nerve-distracting habits predispose her to revery, meditation, and morbid habits of mind and feeling. These shade her soul with gloom which slowly but surely sinks the tone of her health and shatters her constitution. Many a young woman plants the seeds of consumption in some early sorrow, and many more sink the tone of their health to a low degree by desponding reveries and half-despairing longings for something they have but half conceived in their own minds, and put forth no efforts to obtain. It is a burning shame to our nation and age that our women are so impotent and sickly. We believe the best medicine for them would be one that would set them all into a hearty laugh, taken once an hour through the day. They need more sprightly activity, more exhilaration of mind and body, more sunshine and bird-song, more exuberant freshness of life and Happiness. Every gloomy thought is a tax on health. Every desponding hour extracts a year's vitality from the system. A melancholy spirit is like a humor in the blood, breeding a perpetual disease. Doubts and fears are like chills and fevers, which shake and shatter the vital economy to its center. No unhappy woman can enjoy perfect health. The most vigorous constitutions will quail and sink under the weight of a desponding mind. Health! what is all the world without it? Who would sacrifice it for every earthly good? Then let young women beware how they tamper with it by giving way to or cherishing gloomy moods of mind. Seek to be peaceful, cheerful, happy, if you would be well.

Their despondency of mind is equally destructive of spiritual health. It unbalances all the mental powers, gives a morbid activity to some, and a kind of reversed action to others. No gloomy spirit is beautiful or harmonious. We may pity it, but we can not admire it—scarcely love it. In God's sight its sadness is an imperfection—in many instances it is sinfulness. The piety of such a mind is of a questionable character, and its virtue is liable to be tinctured with selfishness or other evils. Its judgment is improved. God loves a cheerful spirit, a happy soul. It is not only a duty we owe to ourselves, but to God, to be happy. Our efforts to subdue every desponding tendency in our minds should be as great and as constant as to master our selfish passions or animal desires. I fully believe we have the power to be happy if we will, or, at least, the most of us have. Some unfortunate minds are constitutionally down in the mouth. Poor things! They suffer a great hereditary evil. They are too hopeless, from a defect in the structure of their minds; but these are few and far between. The rule is, that we may be happy if we will. None of the common allotments and evils in life are absolute barriers in our way. A resolute will and steady purpose, with a proper time, will overcome all. Then buckle on the armor of life, oh, young woman, and rouse your spirit to its best efforts to lead a cheerful and useful life. Let no misfortune weigh you down, but rise above all, and great will be your reward.

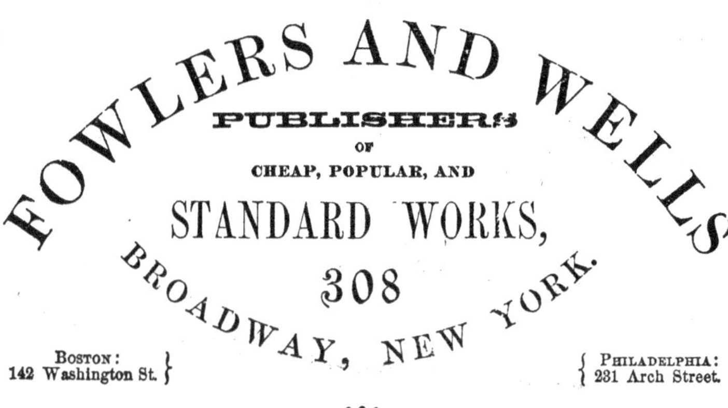

IN order to accommodate "The People" residing in all parts of the United States, the Publishers will forward by return of the FIRST MAIL, any book named in this List. The postage will be prepaid by them at the New York Post-Office. By this arrangement of paying postage in advance, fifty per cent. is saved to the purchaser. The price of each work, including postage, is given, so that the exact amount may be remitted. Fractional parts of a dollar may be sent in postage-stamps. All letters containing orders should be post-paid, and directed as follows: **FOWLERS AND WELLS, 308 Broadway, New York.**

WORKS ON PHRENOLOGY.

AMERICAN PHRENOLOGICAL JOURNAL. A REPOSITORY OF Science, Literature, and General Intelligence; Devoted to Phrenology, Physiology, Education, Mechanism, Agriculture, and to all those Progressive Measures which are calculated to Reform, Elevate, and Improve Mankind. Illustrated with Numerous Engravings. Quarto, suitable for binding. 288 pp. Published Monthly, at One Dollar a Year.

It may be termed the standard authority in all matters pertaining to Phrenology, while the beautiful typography of the Journal, and the superior character of the numerous illustrations, are not exceeded in any work with which we are acquainted.—*American Courier, Phila.*

COMBE'S LECTURE ON PHRENOLOGY. BY GEORGE COMBE. WITH Notes, an Essay on the Phrenological Mode of Investigation, and an Historical Sketch. By Andrew Boardman, M.D. 12mo., 391 pp. Illustrated. Muslin, $1 25.

CHART, FOR RECORDING THE VARIOUS PHRENOLOGICAL DEVELopments. Illustrated with Engravings. Designed for the use of Phrenologists. Price, 6 cts.

CONSTITUTION OF MAN, CONSIDERED IN RELATION TO EXTERNAL Objects. By George Combe. The only authorized American Edition. With Twenty Engravings, and a Portrait of the Author. Paper, 62 cents; Muslin, 87 cents.

THREE HUNDRED THOUSAND COPIES of this great work have been sold, and the demand still increases.

CONSTITUTION OF MAN. BY GEORGE COMBE. ABRIDGED AND Adapted to the Use of Schools, with Questions. To which is added an Appendix descriptive of the Five Principal Races of Men. School Edition, in boards. Price, 30 cents.

The "Constitution of Man" is a work with which every teacher and every pupil should be acquainted. It contains a perfect mine of sound wisdom and enlightened philosophy; and a faithful study of its invaluable lessons would save many a promising youth from a premature grave.—*Journal of Education, Albany, N. Y.*

DEFENCE OF PHRENOLOGY. CONTAINING AN ESSAY ON THE Nature and Value of Phrenological Evidence; also, an able Vindication of Phrenology. By Andrew Boardman. Muslin, 87 cents.

DOMESTIC LIFE. THOUGHTS ON ITS CONCORD AND DISCORD, with Valuable Hints and Suggestions. By N. Sizer. Price, 15 cents.

EDUCATION COMPLETE. EMBRACING PHYSIOLOGY, ANIMAL AND Mental, applied to the Preservation and Restoration of Health of Body and Power of Mind; Self-Culture, and Perfection of Character, including the Management of Youth; Memory and Intellectual Improvement, applied to Self-Education and Juvenile Instruction. By O. S. Fowler. Complete in one large volume. Muslin, $2 50.

Every one should read it who would preserve or restore his health, develop his mind, and improve his character.

EDUCATION: ITS ELEMENTARY PRINCIPLES FOUNDED ON THE Nature of Man. By J. G. Spurzheim, M. D. With an Appendix, containing a Description of the Temperaments, and an Analysis of the Phrenological Faculties. Muslin, 87 cents.

We regard this volume as one of the most important that has been offered to the public for many years. It is full of sound doctrines and practical wisdom.—*Boston Med. and Sur. Jour.*

FAMILIAR LESSONS ON PHRENOLOGY AND PHYSIOLOGY; FOR Children and Youth. Two volumes in one. By Mrs. L. N. Fowler. Muslin, $1 25.

The natural language of each organ is illustrated with wood-cuts, and the work is brought out in a style well adapted to the family circle, as well as the school-room.—*Teachers' Companion.*

LOVE AND PARENTAGE; APPLIED TO THE IMPROVEMENT OF Offspring: including important Directions to Lovers and the Married, concerning the strongest Ties, and most sacred and momentous Relations of Life. By O. S. Fowler. Price, 30 cts.

LOVE, PARENTAGE, AND AMATIVENESS. ONE VOL. MUSLIN, 75 CENTS.

MENTAL SCIENCE. LECTURES ON THE PHILOSOPHY OF PHRENOlogy. By Rev. G. S. Weaver. Illustrated with Engravings Muslin, 87 cents.

These Lectures were prepared for the intellectual, moral, and social benefit of society. The author has, in this respect, done a good work for the rising generation.

MORAL AND INTELLECTUAL SCIENCE; APPLIED TO THE ELEVAtion of Society. By George Combe, Robert Cox, and others. Large octavo. Price, $2 30.

This work contains Essays on Phrenology, as a department of physiological science, exhibiting its varied and important applications to interesting questions of social and moral philosophy, to legislation, medicine, and the arts. With Portraits of Drs. Gall, Spurzheim, and Combe.

MARRIAGE: ITS HISTORY AND PHILOSOPHY. WITH A PHRENOlogical and Physiological Exposition of the Functions and Qualifications necessary for **Happy** Marriages. By L. N. Fowler. Illustrated. Muslin. Price, 75 cents.

It contains a full account of the marriage forms and ceremonies of all nations and tribes, from the earliest history down to the present time. Those who have not yet entered into matrimonial relations should read this book, and all may profit by a perusal,—*N. Y. Illustrated Magazine.*

MEMORY AND INTELLECTUAL INPROVEMENT; APPLIED TO SELF-Education and Juvenile Instruction. By O. S. Fowler. Twentieth Edition. Enlarged and Improved. Illustrated with Engravings. Price, 87 cents.

The science of Phrenology, now so well established, affords us important aid in developing the human mind, according to the natural laws of our being. This, the work before us is pre-eminently calculated to promote, and we cordially recommend it to all.—*Democratic Review.*

MATRIMONY; OR, PHRENOLOGY AND PHYSIOLOGY APPLIED TO the Selection of Congenial Companions for Life; including Directions to the Married for Living together Affectionately and Happily. By O. S. Fowler. Price, 30 cents.

Upwards of sixty thousand copies having been sold in the United States, besides having been republished in London, no man or woman, married or unmarried, should fail to possess a copy.

PHRENOLOGY PROVED, ILLUSTRATED, AND APPLIED; ACCOMPAnied by a Chart, embracing an Analysis of the Primary Mental Powers in their Various Degrees of Development, the Phenomena produced by their Combined Activity, and the Location of the Phrenological Organs in the Head. Together with a View of the Moral and Theological Bearing of the Science. By O. S. and L. N. Fowler. Price, $1 25.

This is a PRACTICAL, STANDARD Work, and may be described as a complete system of the principles and practice of Phrenology. Besides important remarks on the Temperaments, it contains a description of all the primary mental powers, in seven different degrees of development, together with the combinations of the faculties; in short, we regard this work as not only the most important of any which has before been written on the science, but as indispensably necessary to the student who wishes to acquire a thorough knowledge of Phrenological Science.

PHRENOLOGICAL ALMANAC. PUBLISHED ANNUALLY. WITH CALendars for all Latitudes. Profusely Illustrated with Portraits of Distinguished Persons. 6 cts.

POPULAR PHRENOLOGY; EXHIBITING THE PHRENOLOGICAL ADmeasurements of above Fifty Distinguished and Extraordinary Personages of Both Sexes. With numerous Portraits and other Illustrations. By Frederick Coombs. Price, 30 cents.

PHRENOLOGICAL BUST; DESIGNED ESPECIALLY FOR LEARNERS. Showing the Exact Location of all the Organs of the Brain fully developed. Price, including box for packing, $1 25. [May be sent by Express. Not mailable.]

This is one of the most ingenious inventions of the age. A cast made of plaster of Paris, the size of the human head, on which the exact location of each of the Phrenological organs is represented, fully developed, with all the divisions and classifications. Those who cannot obtain the services of a professor may learn in a very short time, from this model head, the science of Phrenology, so far as the location of the organs is concerned.—*N. Y. Sun.*

PHRENOLOGY AND THE SCRIPTURES; SHOWING THEIR HARMONY An able, though small work. By Rev. John Pierpont. Price, 12 cents.

PHRENOLOGICAL GUIDE. DESIGNED FOR STUDENTS OF THEIR own Characters. With numerous illustrative Engravings. Price, 15 cents.

PHRENOLOGY AND PHYSIOLOGY; A SYNOPSIS, COMPRISING A CONdensed Description of the Functions of the Body and Mind. By L. N. Fowler. Price, 15 cts.

CHOLERA: ITS CAUSES, PREVENTION, AND CURE; SHOWING THE Inefficiency of Drug-Treatment, and the Superiority of the Water-Cure in this and in all other Bowel Diseases. By Dr. Shew. Price, 30 cents.

DOMESTIC PRACTICE OF HYDROPATHY, WITH FIFTEEN ENGRAVED Illustrations of Important Subjects, with a Form of a Report for the Assistance of Patients in consulting their Physicians by Correspondence. By Ed. Johnson, M. D. Muslin, $1 50.

EXPERIENCE IN WATER-CURE; A FAMILIAR EXPOSITION OF THE Principles and Results of Water-Treatment in Acute and Chronic Diseases; an Explanation of Water-Cure Processes; Advice on Diet and Regimen, and Particular Directions to Women in the Treatment of Female Diseases, Water-Treatment in Childbirth, and the Diseases of Infancy. Illustrated by Numerous Cases. By Mrs. Nichols. Price, 30 cents.

ERRORS OF PHYSICIANS AND OTHERS IN THE PRACTICE OF THE Water-Cure. By J. H. Rausse. Translated from the German. Price, 30 cents.

HYDROPATHIC FAMILY PHYSICIAN. A READY PRESCRIBER AND Hygienic Adviser, with reference to the Nature, Causes, Prevention and Treatment of Diseases, Accidents, and Casualties of every kind; with a Glossary, Table of Contents, and Index. Illustrated with nearly Three Hundred Engravings. By Joel Shew, M.D. One large volume of 820 pages, substantially bound, in library style. Price, with postage prepaid by mail, $2 50.

It possesses the most practical utility of any of the author's contributions to popular medicine, and is well adapted to give the reader an accurate idea of the organization and functions of the human frame.—*New York Tribune.*

HYDROPATHY FOR THE PEOPLE. WITH PLAIN OBSERVATIONS ON Drugs, Diet, Water, Air, and Exercise. A popular Work, by Wm. Horsell, of London. With Notes and Observations by Dr. Trall. Muslin, 87 cents.

HYDROPATHY: OR, THE WATER-CURE. ITS PRINCIPLES, PROcesses and Modes of Treatment. In part from the most Eminent Authors, Ancient and Modern. Together with an Account of the Latest Methods of Priessnitz. Numerous Cases, with full Treatment described. By Dr. Shew. 12mo. Muslin, $1 25.

HOME TREATMENT FOR SEXUAL ABUSES. A PRACTICAL TREAtise for both Sexes, on the Nature and Causes of Excessive and Unnatural Indulgence, the Diseases and Injuries resulting therefrom, with their Symptoms and Hydropathic Management. By Dr, Trall. Price, 30 cents.

HYDROPATHIC ENCYCLOPÆDIA: A SYSTEM OF HYDROPATHY AND Hygiene. Containing Outlines of Anatomy; Physiology of the Human Body; Hygienic Agencies, and the Preservation of Health; Dietetics, and Hydropathic Cookery; Theory and Practice of Water-Treatment; Special Pathology, and Hydro-Therapeutics, including the Nature, Causes, Symptoms, and Treatment of all known Diseases; Application of Hydropathy to Midwifery and the Nursery. Designed as a Guide to Families and Students, and a Text-Book for Physicians. By R. T. Trall, M. D. Illustrated with upwards of Three Hundred Engravings and Colored Plates. Substantially bound, in one large volume, also in two 12mo. vols. Price for either edition, prepaid by mail, in Muslin, $3 00; in Leather, $3 50.

This is the most comprehensive and popular work yet published on the subject of Hydropathy, with nearly one thousand pages. Of all the numerous publications which have attained such a wide popularity, as issued by Fowlers and Wells, perhaps none are more adapted to general utility than this rich, comprehensive, and well-arranged Encyclopædia.—*N. Y. Tribune.*

HYDROPATHIC QUARTERLY REVIEW. A PROFESSIONAL MAGAzine, devoted to Medical Reform; embracing Articles by the best Writers on Anatomy, Physiology, Pathology, Surgery, Therapeutics, Midwifery, etc.; Reports of Remarkable Cases in General Practice, Criticisms on the Theory and Practice of the various Opposing Systems of Medical Science, Reviews of New Publications of all Schools of Medicine, Reports of the Progress of Health Reform in all its aspects, etc., with appropriate Engraved Illustrations. Terms, a Year, in advance, Two Dollars.

Filled with articles of permanent value which ought to be read by every American.—*N. Y. Trib.*

HYGIENE AND HYDROPATHY. THREE LECTURES. FULL OF Interest and Instruction. By R. S. Houghton, M. D. Price, 30 cents.

INTRODUCTION TO THE WATER-CURE. FOUNDED IN NATURE, AND adapted to the Wants of Man. By Dr. Nichols. Price, 15 cents.

MIDWIFERY, AND THE DISEASES OF WOMEN. A DESCRIPTIVE AND Practical Work, showing the Superiority of Water-Treatment in Menstruation and its Disorders, Chlorosis, Leucorrhœa, Fluor Albus, Prolapsis Uteri, Hysteria, Spinal Diseases and other Weaknesses of Females; in Pregnancy and its Diseases, Abortion, Uterine Hemorrhage, and the General Management of Childbirth, Nursing, etc., etc. Illustrated with Numerous Cases of Treatment. By Joel Shew, M. D. 12mo. 432 pp. Muslin, $1 25.

PARENTS' GUIDE FOR THE TRANSMISSION OF DESIRED QUALITIES to Offspring, and Childbirth made Easy. By Mrs. Hester Pendleton. Price, 60 cents.

PRACTICE OF WATER-CURE. WITH AUTHENTICATED EVIDENCE of its Efficacy and Safety. Containing a detailed account of the various processes used in the Water-Treatment, etc. By James Wilson, M. D., and James M. Gully, M. D. 30 cents.

PHILOSOPHY OF WATER CURE. A DEVELOPMENT OF THE TRUE Principles of Health and Longevity. By John Balbirnie, M. D. With a Letter from Sir Edward Lytton Bulwer. From the Second London Edition. Paper. Price, 30 cents.

PREGNANCY AND CHILDBIRTH. ILLUSTRATED WITH CASES, SHOWing the Remarkable Effects of Water in Mitigating the Pains and Perils of the Parturient State. By Dr. Shew. Paper. Price, 30 cents.

PRINCIPLES OF HYDROPATHY: OR, THE INVALID'S GUIDE TO Health and Happiness. Being a plain, familiar Exposition of the Principles of the Water-Cure System. By David A. Harsha. Price, 15 cents.

RESULTS OF HYDROPATHY; OR, CONSTIPATION NOT A DISEASE of the Bowels, Indigestion not a Disease of the Stomach; with an Exposition of the true Nature and Causes of these Ailments, explaining the reason why they are so certainly cured by the Hydropathic Treatment. By Edward Johnson, M. D. Muslin. Price, 87 cents.

SCIENCE OF SWIMMING. GIVING A HISTORY OF SWIMMING, AND Instructions to Learners. By an Experienced Swimmer. Illustrated with Engravings. 15 cts.

Every boy in the nation should have a copy, and learn to swim.

WATER-CURE LIBRARY. (IN SEVEN 12MO. VOLUMES.) EMBRACING the most popular works on the subject. By American and European Authors. Bound in Embossed Muslin, Library Style. Price, prepaid by mail, only $7 00.

This library comprises most of the important works on the subject of Hydropathy. The volumes are of uniform size and binding, and the whole form a most valuable medical library.

WATER-CURE IN AMERICA. OVER THREE HUNDRED CASES OF various Diseases treated with Water by Drs. Wesselhœft, Shew, Bedortha, Trall, and others. With Cases of Domestic Practice. Designed for Popular as well as Professional Reading. Edited by a Water Patient. Muslin, $1 25.

WATER AND VEGETABLE DIET IN CONSUMPTION, SCROFULA, Cancer, Asthma, and other Chronic Diseases. In which the Advantages of Pure Water are particularly considered. By William Lambe, M. D. With Notes and Additions by Joel Shew, M. D. 12mo. 258 pp. Paper, 62 cents; Muslin, 87 cents.

WATER-CURE APPLIED TO EVERY KNOWN DISEASE. A NEW Theory. A Complete Demonstration of the Advantages of the Hydropathic System of Curing Diseases; *showing also the fallacy of the Allopathic Method, and its Utter Inability to* Effect a Permanent Cure. With Appendix, containing *Hydropathic Diet, and Rules for* Bathing. By J. H. Rausse. Translated from the German. Muslin, 87 cents.

WATER-CURE MANUAL. A POPULAR WORK, EMBRACING Descriptions of the Various Modes of Bathing, the Hygienic and Curative Effects of Air, Exercise, Clothing, Occupation, Diet, Water-Drinking, etc. Together with Descriptions of Diseases, and the Hydropathic Remedies. By Joel Shew, M. D. Muslin. Price, 87 cents.

WATER-CURE ALMANAC. PUBLISHED ANNUALLY, CONTAINING Important and Valuable Hydropathic Matter. Illustrated with Numerous Engravings, with correct calculations for all latitudes. 48 pp. Price, 6 cents.

WATER-CURE JOURNAL, AND HERALD OF REFORMS. DEVOTED TO Physiology, Hydropathy, and the Laws of Life and Health. Illustrated with Numerous Engravings. Quarto. Published Monthly, at $1 00 a Year, in advance.

We know of no American periodical which presents a greater abundance of valuable information on all subjects relating to human progress and welfare.—*N. Y. Tribune.*
This is, unquestionably, the most popular Health Journal in the world.—*N. Y. Evening Post.*

FOWLERS AND WELLS have all works on PHYSIOLOGY, HYDROPATHY, PHRENOLOGY, and the Natural Sciences generally. Booksellers supplied on the most liberal terms. AGENTS wanted in every State, county, and town. These works are universally popular, and thousands might be sold where they have never yet been introduced.

Letters and other communications should, in ALL CASES, be post-paid, and directed to the Publishers, as follows:

FOWLER AND WELLS, 308 Broadway, New York.

MESMERISM AND PSYCHOLOGY.

A NEW AND COMPLETE LIBRARY OF MESMERISM AND PSYCHOLOGY, embracing the most popular works on the subject, with suitable Illustrations. In two volumes of about 900 pp. Bound in Library Style. Price, $3 00.

BIOLOGY; OR, THE PRINCIPLES OF THE HUMAN MIND. DEDUCED from Phys'cal Laws, and on the Voltaic Mechanism of Man. Illustrated. Price, 30 cents.

ELECTRICAL PSYCHOLOGY, PHILOSOPHY OF. IN A COURSE OF Twelve Lectures. By John Bovee Dods. Muslin. Price, 87 cents.

FASCINATION; OR, THE PHILOSOPHY OF CHARMING. ILLUSTRATing the Principles of Life, in connection with Spirit and Matter. By J. B. Newman, M.D. 87 cts.

MENTAL ALCHEMY. A TREATISE ON THE MIND, NERVOUS SYSTEM, Psychology, Magnetism, Mesmerism, and Diseases. By B. B. Williams, M.D. Price, 62 cts.

MACROCOSM AND MICROCOSM; OR, THE UNIVERSE WITHOUT AND the Universe Within: in the World of Sense, and the World of Soul. By Wm. Fishbough. Price, Paper, 62 cents. Muslin, 87 cents.

PHILOSOPHY OF MESMERISM. SIX LECTURES. WITH AN INTROduction. By Rev. John Bovee Dods. Paper. Price, 30 cents.

PSYCHOLOGY; OR, THE SCIENCE OF THE SOUL. CONSIDERED Physiologically and Philosophically. With an Appendix containing Notes of Mesmeric and Psychical Experience. By Joseph Haddock, M. D. With Engravings. Price, 30 cents

SPIRITUAL INTERCOURSE, PHILOSOPHY OF. BEING AN EXPLANAtion of Modern Mysteries. By Andrew Jackson Davis. Price, 62 cents.

SUPERNAL THEOLOGY, AND LIFE IN THE SPHERES. DEDUCED from alleged Spiritual Manifestations. By Owen G. Warren. Octavo. Price 30 cents.

MISCELLANEOUS.

BOTANY FOR ALL CLASSES. CONTAINING A FLORAL DICTIONARY, and a Glossary of Scientific Terms. Illustrated. By J. B. Newman, M.D. Price, 87 cents.

CHEMISTRY, AND ITS APPLICATIONS TO AGRICULTURE AND Commerce. By Justus Liebig, M. D., F. R. S. Price, 25 cents.

DELIA'S DOCTORS; OR, A GLANCE BEHIND THE SCENES. BY Hannah Gardner Creamer. Paper. Price, 62 cents. Muslin, 87 cents.

FAMILIAR LESSONS ON ASTRONOMY: DESIGNED FOR THE USE of Children and Youth in Schools and Families. By Mrs. L. N. Fowler, Illustrated. 87 cts.

FUTURE OF NATIONS: IN WHAT CONSISTS ITS SECURITY. A Lecture delivered in the Tabernacle, New York. By Kossuth. With a Likeness. Price, 12 cts. WHAT THE SISTER ARTS TEACH AS TO FARMING. AN ADDRESS. By Horace Greeley. Price, 12 cents. TRUE BASIS OF AMERICAN INDEPENDENCE. AN ADDRESS. By Hon. Wm. H. Seward. Price, 12 cents. ESSAY ON WAGES. The Means Employed for Upholding Them. By P. C. Friese. Price, 15 cts. LABOR, ITS HISTORY AND PROSPECTS. By Robert Dale Owen. Price, 30 cents.

HINTS TOWARDS REFORMS; CONSISTING OF LECTURES, ESsays, Addresses, and other Writings. With the Crystal Palace, and its Lessons. Second Edition, Enlarged. By Horace Greeley. Price, $1 25.

HOPES AND HELPS FOR THE YOUNG OF BOTH SEXES. RELATING to the Formation of Character, Choice of Avocation, Health, Amusement, Music, Conversation, Cultivation of Intellect, Moral Sentiments, Social Affection, Courtship and Marriage. By Rev. G. S. Weaver. Price, in Paper, 62 cents. Muslin, [illegible] cents.

HUMAN RIGHTS, AND THEIR POLITICAL GUARANTIES. BY Judge Hurlbut. With Notes, by George Combe. Price, Paper, 62 cents. Muslin, 87 cts.

HOME FOR ALL. A NEW, CHEAP, CONVENIENT, AND SUPERIOR Mode of Building, containing full Directions for Constructing Gravel Walls. With Views, Plans, and Engraved Illustrations. New Edition, Revised and Enlarged. Price, 87 cents.

IMMORTALITY TRIUMPHANT. THE EXISTENCE OF A GOD AND Human Immortality, Practically Considered, and the Truth of Divine Revelation Substantiated. By Rev. John Bovee Dods. Price, Paper, 62 cents. Muslin, 87 cents.

LITERATURE AND ART. BY S. MARGARET FULLER. TWO PARTS in one volume. With an Introduction, by Horace Greeley. Muslin. Price, $1 25.

PHONOGRAPHIC TEACHER. PRICE, 45 CENTS. REPORTERS' MANual. 75 cents. And all other Works on Phonography. Wholesale and Retail.

POWER OF KINDNESS; INCULCATING THE PRINCIPLES OF Benevolence and Love. By Charles Morley. Paper, 30 cents. Muslin, 50 cents.

POPULATION, THEORY OF. DEDUCED FROM THE GENERAL LAW of Animal Fertility. With an Introduction by R. T. Trall, M. D. Price, 15 cents.

WOMAN; HER EDUCATION AND INFLUENCE. BY MRS. HUGO Reid. With an Introduction by Mrs. C. M. Kirkland. With Portraits. Price, 87 cents.

THESE works may be ordered in large or small quantities. A liberal discount will be made to AGENTS, and others, who buy to sell again. They may be sent by Express, or as Freight, by Railroad, Steamships, Sailing Vessels, by Stage or Canal, to any City, Town, or Village, in the United States, the Canadas, to Europe, or any place on the Globe.

Checks or drafts, for large amounts, on New York, Philadelphia, or Boston, always preferred. We pay cost of exchange. All letters should be post-paid, and addressed as follows;

FOWLER AND WELLS, 308 Broadway, New York.

www.ingramcontent.com/pod-product-compliance
Lightning Source LLC
LaVergne TN
LVHW050521100826
845148LV00002B/412

* 9 7 8 1 4 2 5 5 2 0 0 0 7 *